Y0-DOM-871

So Why Do I Need
The BIBLE?

So Why Do I Need
The BIBLE?

The Bible is worth becoming excited about
because it is so relevant to everything
that happens between Sundays.
Leave mediocrity behind and move
into a cutting edge walk with God.

CLAYTON DOUGAN

SO WHY DO I NEED THE BIBLE?
By Clayton Dougan
Copyright © 2009
GOSPEL FOLIO PRESS
All Rights Reserved

Published by
GOSPEL FOLIO PRESS
304 Killaly St. W.
Port Colborne, ON L3K 6A6
CANADA

ISBN: 9781926765044
Cover design by Rachel Brooks

All Scripture quotations from the
New American Standard Version unless otherwise noted.

Printed in Canada

Table of Contents

Dedication

Isobel, my cherished wife and partner in life and ministry for more than four decades, selflessly and sacrificially fulfilled the more difficult calling of being married to a traveling evangelist. No man could ask for more; no woman could be more dedicated.

Acknowledgements

I want to express heartfelt thanks to my daughter-in-law Pamela Dougan for the many hours of painstaking work checking and correcting the manuscript and making valuable suggestions.

Pastor Roy Cowieson did me a great service in reading the manuscript from a pastor's point of view. I am grateful for his thoughts and helpful suggestions.

I thank my wife Isobel for her constant encouragement while I was writing.

David Nadeau's patience and professional expertise in editing the manuscript has been invaluable. I thank him. He truly is the "friendly editor."

Many thanks are due to Dr. Michael Horie for his patience and expertise in helping me cope with the finer points of computer use in preparing the manuscript.

Thank you to Bert Boyd, a Board Director of Evangelism International for help in working through the business side of preparing this book for publication.

Introduction

One of my great regrets is that I spent so much time in ministry and not enough in the study of God's Word. One of my greatest joys in life is the time spent alone digging into Holy Scripture. There is nothing so deeply satisfying as that special moment when the Bible comes alive. All else is forgotten when the Holy Spirit has made the meaning of some particular scripture real. It is the knowledge that a very deep need has been met, an inner thirst has been satisfied; that I have met with God. It is a moment when, no matter what is going on in life, darkness is dispelled. When you walk in the light of the conscious presence of God, it takes on a deeply personal meaning. As a child of God, you can enjoy the very reason for being—having a relationship with your Creator.

It is not hard to see why, in the reading and study of God's Word, we are touching the area of the greatest spiritual conflict in the life of any follower of Jesus. Being a follower of Jesus, by definition, means to *turn from darkness to light and from the dominion of Satan to God"* (Acts 26:18). The enemy, Satan, does not give up easily. His constant strategy is to keep you, as a believer in Jesus, from enjoying the peace and confidence of walking with God. Without doubt, keeping you from the prayerful, meditative, and obedient study of God's Word is the area of Satan's most concentrated efforts.

He knows well that your disciplined study of the Word is the only way you can grow in your union with Christ. Through planned strategy the enemy comes against God's people (2 Cor. 2:11; Eph. 6:11).

From the beginning of time the devil has demonstrated that he is the master of deception. From Adam and Eve in the Garden of Eden, down through the generations, his tactics have been to deceive. He is described as Satan who deceives the whole world (Rev. 12:9). Today, his deception comes in the areas of *"the lust of the flesh and the lust of the eyes and the boastful pride of life"* (1 Jn. 2:16). Genesis 3:6 shows what a smooth operator he is: *"When the woman saw that the tree was good for food and that it was a delight to the eyes and that the tree was desirable to make one wise, she took from its fruit and ate; and she gave also to her husband with her, and he ate."* This has been his method ever since.

There is nothing more sad or grieving to God's heart than when any of His children do something to give others reason to question our claims. Saying our past has been forgiven and our lives have been transformed by the power of the Holy Spirit and that heaven is our home is quite a mouthful. Why is it that so many of us who claim so much, live as if we did not really believe those claims? It is because the devil's deception is working. His strategy has us go through the motions without the life-changing power. He has us in defeat instead of victory.

The last thing this writer wants to do is to sit in judgment on fellow-followers of Jesus. The temptations in life are enormous; I am deeply aware of past failures and personal weakness. Only the reality of Jesus living inside us by the Holy Spirit can give us the power to be overcomers, to stand strong with integrity and purity. It is through the prayerful study of the Bible that we see and begin to utilize the resources at our disposal. Because all Scripture is inspired by God (literally God-breathed), it opens to us a whole new world of light instead of darkness, assurance instead of doubt, peace instead of panic, hope instead of fear and uncertainty.

At the end of 2004 I had the privilege of being part of a team visiting northern Uganda, southern Sudan and Kenya. Daniel Greeve, a young Canadian in his early twenties, was part of the team. During the trip God taught Daniel many things; it was especially exciting to see his love for God's Word rise to new heights. Here is some of his testimony: "I never would have

thought that the longer you spend in personal devotion, the better it gets!"

It is my earnest prayer that through this book you will experience the sheer delight that comes from the discovery—or rediscovery—of God's Word.

ONE

From Head to Heart

The memory is vivid. The impact of that moment was powerful and life changing. The result was a healing, a releasing from a poor self-image. It meant greater victory where there had been failure and defeat. It meant no longer constantly questioning who I really am. It meant a new quality of life, a clearer vision for the future, and a greater sense of purpose combined with significantly increased effectiveness and fruitfulness in following Jesus. The thing no one can live without—assured hope and peace of mind—became real. What is this monumental it? I refer to discovering that being a real Christian means Jesus Christ really lives inside me by the Holy Spirit. This is something far more than a head matter, it is a truth that dawns upon the mind and explodes in the inner being, transforming life. It begins with the most intimately personal things and progresses to family relationships, work ethic, and leisure time; to every facet of life. Where is such a discovery made? It is made in one of those priceless moments when the Holy Spirit lights up the truth of God's Word and the hungry, the searching, the spiritually bankrupt soul sees what God is really getting at.

I first encountered this life-changing truth while helping in an evangelistic event in the north of England. The evangelist leading the team encouraged us to spend some time each morning in reading and study. Part of my reading was in the old book by Andrew Murray, "Abide in Christ". It is basically teaching on John chapter 15. I'll never forget that, as I read and studied John chapter15, the truth began to dawn upon me that, just as fruit on a vine is produced as a result of the life of the vine flowing through the branches, so the beautiful fruit of the Holy Spirit is produced in my life through Christ's life in me, flowing through me. Jesus says in John 15, *"I am the vine, you are the branches; he who abides in Me and I in him, he bears much fruit, for apart from Me you can do nothing."* I began to discover then that serving the Lord Jesus is not what I can do for Him, but rather what He can do in and through me.

Around that time I was developing a serious relationship with the girl who is now my wife. Her dad, the late Jim Foggo, was a shoemaker by trade. Many a rich hour I spent in his workshop while he mended shoes. He shared from the depth of his knowledge of God's Word. He helped me so much in developing my understanding of the fact that Christ lives on the inside of me desiring to live through my surrendered life.

Christ is everywhere in the Bible and the whole point of us having the Bible in our own language is so we can discover the historical Jesus for ourselves and be forever impacted by what He did on our behalf. Without exaggerating, this is the primary reason the Holy Spirit lives inside every true believer in Jesus. His function is to show us the uniqueness, the magnificence, and the life-changing power of our Saviour. He also shows that the relationship a real Christian has with Jesus means that Jesus becomes more than the giver of life. The Christian's body becomes the instrument by which Jesus lives His life today.

Reference was made earlier to the spiritually bankrupt soul; one where there is no real joy, victory over sin or effectiveness in service. In other words, where life has become rather mechanical. This is a concept we all have difficulty with, yet it is of vital importance. This writer is the first to acknowledge that he has a problem being willing to come to grips with what he sees when he takes a totally honest look at his own heart and the evil he is capable of. Taking such a look at the real me in the uncompromising light of God's perfect holiness is a truly unnerving experience. Some would say that, for the truly liberated mind, there is no absolute right or wrong; we are free to set our own standards. However, when totally honest before God, that position cannot be taken. I have to acknowledge that, apart from the unconditional love and the unbelievable grace of God, I am a spiritually bankrupt soul. Allow me to simply say: if Jesus is who He claimed to be—the Son of God—and if we consider His impact on human history, then God is someone we simply cannot ignore. What God wants to do in our lives goes far beyond positive thinking and being what we believe we can be. It is not possible for us to conceive of all God has for us because of Jesus. He has in mind you being someone you never could be apart from Him. In comparison, every possible human idea regarding what we could make of ourselves is utter bankruptcy.

Coming back to our theme: all we can know about the supernatural God and the supernatural life He offers as a gift, we discover in this supernatural Word of God, the Bible. The Bible shows me that my real inner condition, compared to God's purity, can only be described as total spiritual bankruptcy—sinfulness. The Bible shows me that Jesus, being the antithesis of everything I am naturally, is able to transform my situation. When I see the awfulness of the real me, I cannot hope to have any kind of relationship with my Creator because light and darkness have nothing in common. They cannot co-exist. I deserve to be banished from God forever; and would be, apart from Jesus. Jesus took the awfulness of my real sinful self upon Himself, suffered my banishment and the judgment I deserved. He submitted to God's will by dying in my place. The historical resurrection of Jesus from the dead is what gives significance to what He did on the cross. It gives meaning far beyond the merely religious. It means He really is the Son of God, the only one able to deal with my spiritual bankruptcy.

It has to be remembered that the bodily resurrection of Jesus is not the product of the Christian church but its foundation. The early disciples proclaimed the resurrection right under the noses of the people who had crucified Jesus and in full view of the empty tomb. No body was produced; that would have been simple to do, had He not risen. All but one of His apostles gave their lives as martyrs in the service of the risen Jesus; people don't die for something they know is not true. The resurrection of Jesus resulted in the transformation of the first disciples. Jesus has been transforming people ever since. The resurrection is the fulfilment of prophecies made hundreds of years before the event.

The challenge is: are we willing to see ourselves as God sees us and to acknowledge our spiritual bankruptcy? Are we willing to have a complete change of mind (repentance) toward our sinful condition? Are we willing to turn to Jesus and renounce our bankrupt and self-centred lifestyle? This is conversion. Are we willing to trust, not what we think we can do but rather, what Jesus has done on our behalf as the only way we can be brought out of our hopeless spiritual bankruptcy into a right relationship with God. Are we willing to make Jesus absolute Lord of our lives and to be filled with the Holy Spirit so we are able to walk in absolute obedience to God's Word? An example of this kind of obedience is in acting on the command of Jesus and on the example of early believers to believe and be baptised.

Thus begins an ongoing, ever-growing new life, full of purpose and hope in relationship with God and with His people, your new family, His church.

A word for those who may be believers in Jesus but whose walk with Him has known better days. There is no more unhappy person than the one who once walked closely with the Lord Jesus but who, for whatever reason, has allowed something or someone to distract them. This distraction may have come through a wrong or unhelpful relationship in marriage, in an extramarital affair, or in lowered standards in business practice. It may have come through the pressures of life and family, causing you to drift spiritually. Maybe you had a deeply hurtful or trying experience, which has caused anger or disillusionment. So you took your eyes off the One you were following, the Lord Jesus Christ.

You may be reading this book out of a deep-seated desire to be where you know you ought to be, enjoying the presence and power of Jesus. You know, no matter what, there ought to be an inner peace that cannot be touched by changing circumstances. I have known what it means to be in church every Sunday, to be involved in Christian service, and all the time to be estranged from Jesus, to be as cold as ice inside. I have seen joy, peace, and harmony restored to a family when the husband and father was renewed in his relationship to Jesus after many years of bad choices and drifting. The bad choices involved allowing being hurt by others to grow into deep resentment. This resulted in drifting into a very unhappy life style. The tragedy is, things like this do not need to happen.

We can do nothing about the consequences of bad choices, but God's love is unconditional, His forgiveness complete, and His presence for every moment guaranteed. The good news is that God is in the business of restoring His broken and erring children.

A word about being filled with the Holy Spirit: If He is not filling us, the Bible remains a closed book. Without the Holy Spirit, reading or studying the Bible is but an academic exercise. The purpose of this book is to help you get beyond the merely intellectual to a deep and meaningful ongoing relationship with Jesus. If you are not filled with the Holy Spirit, you won't even want to read the Bible. It is a sad fact that a large percentage of today's Christians do not read the Bible on a regular basis. The losses for such people are incalculable. There is no longer the sense of the nearness of Jesus, which so often leads to defeat by personal sin. Compromising with society's thinking, which has no place for God or His Word, also becomes an issue.

For the purposes of this book we will confine ourselves to the foundational details of being filled with the Holy Spirit. It is important to bear in mind we cannot make a doctrine out of an experience. As Oswald Chambers once said, "Let God be as original with other people as He is with you." We are talking about the ongoing experience of allowing the Holy Spirit to be in us and to fill our lives like a well of water springing up to eternal life (John 4.14). If this is not a reality in our experience, the Bible remains a closed book. Jesus said again: *"When the Spirit of truth comes, He will guide you into all truth"* (John 16.13). Surrendering your life to Jesus as Lord so you can be filled with the Holy Spirit is what makes the Bible come alive. Only then will you be willing to submit to its authority. Only then will your spiritual appetite grow. God's Word will become food for your hungry soul, water to quench your thirst in the dryness of the spiritual desert around you. You will no longer be in a rut but in that exciting place of knowing you are learning to live as you were meant to live. It will not be in the deadness of mere religion but in the freshness of a wonderful relationship with your Creator.

When it comes to the how to of being filled with the Holy Spirit, no one has put it more simply or more profoundly than the late Dr. A.W. Tozer: (quotes from Dr. Tozer are in italics)

- *Be sure you can be filled with the Holy Spirit. Being filled with the Holy Spirit is not some special, deluxe edition of Christianity.* Speaking of Jesus death at Calvary he says, *there was included, as a purchase of that blood, your right to a full, Spirit-filled life.*

- *Before you can be filled with the Spirit you must desire to be filled.* It is very important to realise what is involved. The Holy Spirit filling your life means Jesus is living His life on the inside of you. *That Spirit, if He ever possesses you, will be the Lord of your life.* You must realize that the world you live in every day is opposed to the presence of the Holy Spirit. His presence in you has the effect of making you able to be what Jesus called salt and light in the world. This will have the effect of exposing the darkness and sin around you, something human nature hates to happen. This is where ridicule and persecution begin.

- *Are you sure you need to be filled?* Perhaps after years of what you know to be mediocrity, with little joy in sharing your faith with others, with no real passion for God's Word and with more defeat than victory in the area of personal sin, there is a deep longing for that touch from God on your life. If you are really there, then you are sure you need to be filled with the Holy Spirit. What a wonderful place to be. God has great things in store for you.

Dr. Tozer gives three simple steps to follow. On the surface they appear to be small steps but, in the context of the rest of your life, they are giant leaps.

First: *"Present your body a living and holy sacrifice, acceptable to God which is your spiritual service of worship"* (Rom. 12:1). So long as we persist in keeping areas of our lives for ourselves and refuse to give up all rights to ourselves, we will never be filled with the Holy Spirit. God will fill whatever is emptied and given totally to Him.

Second: Ask God to fill you with His Spirit. God's promise is to be taken at face value and acted upon in faith. Remember, it is impossible for God to break His promises. His promise is, *"Ask, and it will be given to you; seek, and you will find; knock, and it will be opened to you. If you then, being evil, know how to give good gifts to your children, how much more will your heavenly Father give the Holy Spirit to those who ask Him?"* (Luke 11:9-13).

Third: Are you ready to obey and do what you are asked to do? Acts 5:32 speaks of *"...the Holy Spirit whom God has given to those who obey Him."* A huge part of the thrill of either discovering or rediscovering the Bible is that God is going to show us His design, as creator, for how life should be lived. In the end, it all comes down to whether or not you and I are willing to be fully surrendered to Him, to take Him at His word and to obey what He asks us to do.

When the implications of surrendering our bodies to God, sincerely asking Him to fill us, and being willing to obey Him without question begin to dawn on us, we suddenly realise there is a huge exercise of the will involved. I wrestled with this for a long time before surrendering to Jesus as Lord, having come to a complete end of myself and my resources.

My first year in ministry, after Bible School, was a complete disaster, humanly speaking. Just about everything that could go wrong, went wrong. The word discouragement took on a whole new meaning for me, so much so that I left ministry and went back to banking. There followed some months of a compromising life style. I was kidding myself that I could go through all the motions of being a Jesus-follower, all the time making excuses for my compromising and, I have to say, personal defeat. Unexpectedly I had a time in hospital which meant I had plenty of time to think. That is when it dawned on me I had made a terrible mistake. I had run away from my true calling. What was I to do? As far as I was concerned, I had blown it very badly. I was on the scrap heap and all washed up, as far as my calling was concerned. While I was at my lowest, the Sunday sermon one week was from the book of Jonah, chapter three and verse one, *"the word of the Lord came to Jonah the second time."* If you know the story of Jonah, you will know that he too had run away from what he knew to be God's call on his life. The sermon that day was about the fact that God gave Jonah a second chance. Its impossible to express adequately the healing that touched me. In my brokenness and defeat I was overwhelmed with God's love for me. He had not, after all, abandoned me on the scrap heap. I saw then, as I had never seen before, that the key to my walk with God was absolute abandonment of myself to Him, so that He could do in me and through me what He wanted to do, and in the manner He wanted it done. By the grace of God Isobel and I went back to where we had left off. We began again, in other words. Through bitter experience I was learning that my effectiveness was all a matter of the Lord Jesus living His life in me and then operating through me. In other words being filled with the Holy Spirit.

When we talk about following Jesus, being His disciples, we are talking about radical action resulting in radical change leading to a radical lifestyle. Are you looking for that quality of life you know must be there somewhere but which has eluded you? It is a quality of life which is far better than anything this world has to offer. This is it:

- Humbling yourself at the feet of the Saviour who loved you and took on Himself all your sin, failure, and guilt when He died for you.

- Surrendering your will to Him as Lord so He can fill you with His Holy Spirit. This means Jesus living His life inside you, reproducing Himself through you. This is what the Bible calls the fruit of the Spirit. Jesus did not only die for you and me; He rose for us as well. The resurrection does not just mean Jesus rose from the dead historically; it means He is still alive.

- The coming of the Holy Spirit means resurrection life can now be lived through surrendered individuals.

In the second half of the seventh century BC the young King Josiah reigned in Jerusalem as the seventeenth king of Judah. From the beginning of his reign he made up his mind to walk with God. He became king after a particularly sad time in his people's history—they had completely abandoned their heritage as the people of God. The turning point came when this young king's commitment to walk with God led to the rediscovery of God's Word. This event led to a great self-humbling on the part of the king and his people and brought an immediate response from God: *"Because your heart was tender and you humbled yourself before the Lord when you heard what I spoke and you have torn your clothes and you have wept before Me, I truly have heard you, declares the Lord"* (2 Kgs. 22:19). This is radical. A changed leader led to a changed nation. If you are in any position of leadership as you read this book but you are leading in the bankruptcy of your self-sufficiency and you know it is not working, heed the example of King Josiah.

I met Len while pastoring in Eastbourne, England. A cynical old sailor, Len was persuaded by his niece to visit the church. The first time he walked through the doors he was warmly welcomed by a older member who was a true Jesus-follower, a keen Bible student, and a man who was passionate about introducing others to Jesus. Within a short time Len's new friend had introduced him to the Lord Jesus; this resulted in what can only be described as a radical change in Len's life. I loved making pastoral visits to his tiny apartment. The thing that stands out was how Len, only a short time previously, would have scoffed at the whole idea of reading the Bible. He developed a deep love for God's Word. Every time I visited, his Bible was open on the kitchen table and he would eagerly share the things the Holy Spirit was teaching him. The thrill remained with Len to the end of his life.

You may be in leadership in business, politics, church, or a well-known ministry. It could be you have never come to faith in Christ or that your personal walk with God has seen better times and can no longer be described as radical, cutting edge, or even warm. There is not a more unhappy person than the one, (I trust I am not describing you) whose love for Jesus has grown cold or who is mechanically trying to serve God. Such a person cannot stand being around people who are truly filled with the Holy Spirit, people who are more fruitful than frothy. Nor can they find happiness in relationships with people who have never loved Jesus because they know that that lifestyle can never totally meet the deepest needs of the heart. May I encourage you to stop reading right now and, by an act of your will, humble yourself before God, be willing to renounce the cold or old ways and surrender your entire being to Jesus Christ as Lord. Ask Him to make you clean as you trust what He has done for you rather than what you can do for yourself. Ask Him to fill you with His Holy Spirit. Even if you see yourself as just an ordinary person like Len, may I remind you that, in God's sight, you are anything but ordinary. You are created in His image, loved with His unconditional love and redeemed through what Jesus did for you on the cross. Eternal Life is what it is all about and that is what is available to you right now in Christ. That means God's life inside you, being lived through you and becoming your hope for the future even beyond this life. I encourage you to stop reading and take the steps outlined earlier. The results in your life will be just as vital and radical as for anyone else who makes that all-important act of the will in surrendering totally to Jesus Christ as Lord and, as a result, being filled with His Holy Spirit.

As I conclude this chapter may I emphasize again something that cannot be emphasized too strongly, until we know the real meaning of being filled with the Holy Spirit, the Bible will remain a closed book. The Bible is given to us so that in and through it we can, in our lostness, find God and cultivate the greatest of all relationships, the relationship between the Creator and those He created for Himself.

TWO

It's All About Meeting God

The idea that anyone could be God's friend is something you may not have thought much about. Any thought you have given to the matter may simply have been on the, "What a friend we have in Jesus" level; stuff you consider for children in Sunday School. Perhaps seeing yourself in an Abraham-like relationship with God is mere fantasy to you and not to be taken seriously. In your mind the whole concept is worlds away from affecting what real life is all about. "Let's get real," do I hear you say? Your world may be the dog-eat-dog world where survival is the name of the game. God having any relevance to your world may be increasingly difficult to imagine. Where you spend your nine-to-five day, to say nothing about what happens before nine and after five, may be well removed from your present concept of God. You may have a problem relating current or past experience of church to what life is like for you every day. That is why so many churches are in decline. For most people, their church experience, either in worship or in the kind of preaching they hear, or both, has no relevance whatsoever to life during the rest of their week. It could be, however, that you have the conviction, deep inside, that there is more to the whole idea than you are currently experiencing. Whatever it is, you long for it.

Abraham's friendship with God needs to be seen, not in terms of him being some super-spiritual, super-human individual, but in terms of the immense greatness of God, the Almighty, who challenged him with the question, *"Is anything too difficult for the Lord?"* (Gen. 18:14). This is the God with whom he had his personal and intimate friendship. It was a friendship which affected the entire direction of Abraham's life, whom he married, the quality of the marriage, his integrity in decision making, how he managed his possessions, and how he handled failure and success. It was front and centre when major decisions were made and when he faced his greatest challenges. The whole thing could be summed up in the phrase which is amazingly simple and yet profound: *"Abraham believed God."* You can read the whole story in Genesis chapters 12 to 25.

I well remember the reaction of my elderly grandmother when one of her daughters, my Aunt Martha, was taking a flight from Scotland to Canada for the first time. Granny had no understanding of either the size or the power of the machine designed for trans-atlantic flight. Aerodynamics were completely foreign to her; the skill and training of the pilot were irrelevant. All she could think about was her daughter flying. Her limited understanding of international travel and her refusal to stop worrying about her Martha meant denying herself the thrill of discovering a whole new world. Martha, on the other hand, had no more understanding of the intricacies of the situation than did Granny. She, in company with many others, was prepared to believe the information she had been given and to act upon it. Her step of faith was not a leap in the dark. She trusted the reliable information and, encouraged by the experience of others, had one of the most enriching experiences of her life.

I take it you have either some knowledge of God or at least a desire to know something about Him or you probably would not be reading a book like this. If we know anything about God, we know He is completely other than we are; He is not confined to time and space. He is unlimited in power (omnipotent), unlimited in knowledge (omniscient) and present everywhere at all times (omnipresent). Whatever we hope to know about God should begin here. Let's face it; any lesser god would come within the limits of human thought and reason. A god with any limits would not be much of a god. How could such a god be trusted implicitly? We must remember that the God of the Bible who wants to be in relationship with humanity is the all mighty Creator, the sovereign Lord of heaven and earth. He says of Himself, *"My thoughts are not your thoughts, nor are your ways*

My ways. For as the heavens are higher than the earth, so are My ways higher than your ways and My thoughts than your thoughts" (Isa. 55:8-9). But the wonder of it all is, you and I are created in His image. As such, we are created to know Him. Being created in His image means we are creative beings; we are spiritual and emotional; we are rational and morally responsible; we appreciate beauty. My wife and I had an old dog. He appreciated beautiful trees, but for a very different reason! The dog's whole existence was governed by instinct. Being created in God's image (see Gen. 1:27), we are "an expression or transcription of the eternal, incorporeal creator in terms of temporal, bodily, creaturely existence—as one might attempt a transcription of a symphony into a sonnet."[1] To speak of knowing God, therefore, is neither simplistic nor an affront to the intellect. When, by an intelligent act of the will, you or I believe God, His side of the friendship—forgiveness, inner transformation, peace, purpose and hope—becomes part of the stuff of life.

Do you truly desire to know God in the kind of relationship He wants to have with you? God is not at all interested in anything superficial. We are dealing with the Creator of the universe. He is the giver of all life. Through what He has done for us in Jesus, the perfect demonstration of what being in God's image means, He offers us eternal life. Please understand, eternal life is His own life. Knowing God means sharing that life. The beginning of 1 John in the New Testament teaches that the Christian is called into fellowship with God and with His Son Jesus Christ. It won't happen on our terms. God as Creator and Redeemer has every right to dictate the terms of the relationship. Whether we like it or not, what happens to us after life on earth is entirely in His hands. This is not something you and I are allowed to have an opinion about. We are faced with a simple choice: we take to heart who God is and what He has done through Jesus to make Himself known to us, or we don't. If we do, we begin a lifestyle built on a constantly growing relationship with our Creator. Think of it again. It means He is

---

1   Derek Kidner, Genesis—an Introduction and Commentary (Tyndale, O.T. Commentaries, IVP)

literally living inside us by the Holy Spirit. That relationship will culminate in the richest of all life in God's immediate presence forever. If we don't, we continue in our sinful, selfish rebellion against God. It may be you are well aware of the kind of dead-end road that that is. Or maybe the deception continues and your own way is still too enjoyable. I gently remind you—it is a deception. Continuing with it means a lifestyle void of any real relationship with your Creator, even if it is a religious lifestyle. This ultimately leads to being separated from God forever because everything hangs on what we do with the Son of God. Jesus Christ, the Son of God, is the Creator's revelation of Himself to the world. He is the expression of the Creator's unconditional love for men and women, even those who choose to walk away from God and who, as a result, are experiencing some of the consequences of that choice. With every choice there are inevitable consequences.

She was a very religious woman, involved in many church-related activities for most of her earlier life. One day it dawned on her that all she had was religious practice. God was still outside her life. She did not know Him personally. Even though the religious practice was good, it was totally self-centred. Not that she was necessarily a selfish person; she did many good works that made her feel good. What she came to realise was she was missing the whole point of the exercise. The whole point was that my mother's life was meant to be God-centred and that could never be achieved by what she was doing for herself, but only by what God had done for her through His Son Jesus. What a day it was in the history of my family when she made a choice to open her life to the Son of God so He could live inside her by the Holy Spirit. The results of that choice go on to this day. It meant my sister and I grew up having the priceless possession of a praying mom. The quality of her life from that day on was a testimony to the reality of the relationship with her Creator. The Bible has a wonderful expression which sums up Mother's life perfectly: *"Christ in you, the hope of glory"* (Col. 1:27). When she passed away, her funeral was a victorious occasion. The historical fact of the resurrection of the Lord Jesus from the dead and the consistent, ongoing change in Mother's life are the things that give us the assurance she is in the presence of Jesus. This is the hope of the Christian.

We are about to embark on the incredible adventure of learning more about how this life-changing relationship with God develops. At the very heart of this adventure is the understanding that God still speaks today through His inspired Word, the Bible. The inspiration of the Bible will be dealt with later; for now, I want to concentrate on the living quality of the Bible. By that I mean its ability to speak to people's lives with relevance and power so that, when acted upon, the effect is truly life-changing. You will become increasingly aware that the deepest areas of personal need are being touched with comfort, challenge, rebuke, and a sense of direction. But above any other effect the Bible's power can have upon life is its ability to reveal God to us. Meeting God in His Word is what it is all about. There is nothing richer or more deeply satisfying. It is so deeply satisfying that you will never get enough. The satisfaction is experienced through the exercise of meeting God and discovering that He is inexhaustible in the richness of who He is and in the abundance of what He wants to pour into your heart by the Holy Spirit. The pursuit of personal wealth, when it is all consuming, leaves the deepest area of your soul empty and unsatisfied. Pornography can also become an addiction so powerful that it can ruin lives, break up families, and leave individuals full of deep regret, shame, and utter emptiness. But meeting God in His Word can fill you with a deep sense of being in vital fellowship with your Creator, and having discovered the reason for being.

Years ago, my marriage almost fell apart, mainly because my ministry as an evangelist became all consuming. There was little time for a relationship with God or with my wife. I was a busy preacher, but was cold as ice in my heart. It was one of the blackest times of my life. Today I am so grateful the Holy Spirit brought me to a place of utter brokenness and deep repentance. I discovered the simple fact of Jesus living inside me and that all there is in God is mine to enjoy. If you are a preacher and you know you are losing your real relationship with God and with your family, humble yourself before God and your spouse; get to the place where God wants you to be. That may not be where you think you should be. So often our preacher ego gets in the way of what God wants. What did I learn because of my difficult time? To read the Bible through once a year. This is the most significant habit I have ever adopted. It's amazing how God's Word speaks to specific situations in my life at just the right time. I received peace in troubled times and a direction in confusing times. It brought healing to my marriage and family.

What gives the Bible its unique quality, such that it remains so alive and relevant for every generation? It is quite a claim the Bible is making for itself when it says, *"For the Word of God is living and active and sharper than any two-edged sword, and piercing as far as the division of soul and spirit, of both joints and marrow, and able to judge the thoughts and intentions of the heart"* (Heb. 4:12). Taking this seriously means realizing why the Bible will remain a closed book unless you come to it with a willingness to have Jesus Christ as Lord in your life so you can be filled with the Holy Spirit. The penetrating power of God's Word means it will touch the deepest and most sensitive areas of your life. It will bring to light what you have hidden and will examine your motives. It will bring immense encouragement where needed and will shed light on your circumstances when you need direction. *"Your Word is a lamp to my feet and a light to my path"* (Ps. 119:105).

Understanding this, we begin to see that the Bible is not an option in the Christian's life, it is indispensable if you want progress and growth. Growing in your relationship with God simply will not happen unless you are serious about God's Word. This is not an academic discussion about mere religious practice because the Bible is the living Word of the living God through which you can find Him and grow in your knowledge of Him.

Speaking of Hebrews 4:12, Prof. F. F. Bruce says,

> "It is not like the word of man; it is living, effective and self-fulfilling; it diagnoses the condition of the human heart, it brings blessing to those

who receive it in faith and pronounces judgement on those who disregard it. That the Word of God probes the inmost recesses of our spiritual being and brings the subconscious motives to light is what is meant...."[2]

It has to be this way. As a follower of Jesus you are told *"your fellowship is with the Father and with His Son Jesus Christ"* (1 Jn. 1:3). That means you are in relationship with Almighty God who is light (1 Jn. 1:5). To make it happen, He has *"called you out of darkness into His marvellous light"* (1 Pet. 2:9). Since God is light and you have been called out of the darkness and since light and darkness cannot coexist, you can see why God probes so deeply. It is no exaggeration to say that very few of us really appreciate the quality of life we could be enjoying or what is really available when we are in relationship with our Creator through Jesus. As a Christian, do you understand that none of the richness of life, none of the available deliverance from the power of our sinful, self-centred lifestyle, and none of the ability to be excited about your hope for the future is possible as long as you live a life of compromise? You must be willing to renounce anything that has anything to do with living in darkness. The only way forward is by allowing Jesus to be Lord in every area of your life. That is why there is no point in churches praying to God for revival if they are not prepared to repent deeply and forsake everything they know is grieving the heart of God. When a church gets to that place, it needs to discover just how powerful God's Word can be in their lives. It is no wonder the area of greatest spiritual conflict for the Christian is with regard to the time given to the prayerful reading and study of God's Word.

When Jesus said things like, *"If you love Me, you will keep My commandments"* (John 14:15), He was saying that real love for Him means total submission to Him as Lord and total obedience to His Word. When God begins that deeper work in your life, to bring you to the moment of complete surrender

---

2   F. F. Bruce, "The Epistle to the Hebrews" (New London Commentaries—Marshall, Morgan & Scott) 81, 82.

to Jesus Christ as Lord, it very often means going the way of brokenness. You know beyond all doubt that God is at work and that what is going on is deeper than anything you have ever experienced. Every area of your darkness is being exposed by the holy light of God's Spirit. Every selfish motive is being brought into the open. Every unconfessed and unforgiven sin becomes an unbearable burden because you realize how such things grieve God's Holy Spirit. Are you overwhelmed with how evil your heart is and how utterly holy God is? With such a realization comes the deep conviction that what is going on has behind it the everlasting, unconditional love of Almighty God. It is impossible to put into words how I felt at that awesome moment when God confronted me with the wonder of His love for me and, by contrast, the coldness of my icy little heart. At that moment I realized my coldness meant there would be no victory over personal sin, no joy or effectiveness in living as a Christian. I could go through the motions, but it was all me working for Jesus, rather than Jesus working in and through me. What a moment when I realized that a true Christian experience was no more than Jesus living His life through me. There came a deep brokenness, total surrender, and the overwhelming sense of the Holy Spirit flooding my entire being. Everything changed. Now it was Him, not me. I had peace. I was free to be me. In the good times and the bad times, God's presence was real. There are still bad times, but how wonderfully freeing it is to know, as a dear friend said, "Sometimes it's OK not to be OK." Those are the times when God's Word is so relevant. Through it I hear what God wants to say to me in the bad times and the Holy Spirit brings peace no matter what.

I have watched this happen in so many others. Our older son began having seizures as a teenager and was told if he remained free of them for a year it could mean he was growing out of them. When the year was almost over, he had another seizure. It was devastating and he became so angry. At the height of his anger he went into his room and opened his Bible. He read, *"Shall we indeed accept good from God and not accept adversity?"* (Job 2:10). The Holy Spirit, through God's Word, changed his heart. From that day to this (twenty years or so on) there has been no anger or complaint, even though he had to come to terms with the fact that there was always going to be the danger of having seizures.

A Challenge

Are you willing, right now, to surrender everything to Jesus Christ as Lord in your life, to be filled with the Holy Spirit; and with His help, commit yourself to the discipline of reading and studying God's Word on a daily basis?

What to Do

Talk to God. Tell Him about the things that have kept you from enjoying Him and His Word. Tell Him you are willing to put them out of your life, if they are legitimate things, to give them their true place in your priority list. Ask Him to fill you with His Holy Spirit as you make Jesus the supreme ruler of your life. The Holy Spirit will create a love for God's Word in your heart. Make it a high priority to set aside a time and place where you can quietly and prayerfully read God's Word, even if it's only five minutes a day to start. Your appetite will grow. As soon as possible, get a help to daily Bible reading.

THREE

How Confident Can I Be in the Bible?

The Bible Is Inspired and Authoritative

The Bible makes an astounding claim for itself. So astounding that, if valid, this claim would make it totally unique. The Bible claims to be literally God-breathed, the out-breathing of God. This expression, God-breathed, is a literal translation of the word inspired. This means every word in the Bible is spoken by the breath of God. This claim comes in 2 Timothy 3:16-17: *"All Scripture is inspired [God-breathed] by God and profitable for teaching, for reproof, for correction, for training in righteousness; so that the man of God may be adequate, equipped for every good work."* Those through whom God breathed His Word were not robots. They maintained their personalities. They were people whom God was able to use. *"Men moved by the Holy Spirit spoke from God"* is how the apostle Peter put it in the New Testament (2 Pet. 1:20-21). Dr. J. I. Packer, speaking about Scripture having a divine origin says,

> "In this sense, inspiration is to be defined as a supernatural, providential influence of God's Holy Spirit upon the human authors which caused them to write what He wished to be written for the communication of revealed truth to others."[3]

---

3   J. I. Packer, "Fundamentalism and the Word of God" (I.V.F) 77

Some of us may have a problem with being expected to believe someone only on the evidence of that person's own testimony. We are talking here about the Bible's testimony about itself. However, we must not be too hasty in jumping to conclusions. We must not simply scrap the whole idea of the inspiration of Scripture merely because it is Scripture making the claim for itself. It is important to remember that the evidence of any person giving testimony about themselves is of crucial importance and must be listened to. It would be dishonest to rest your case on evidence, either for or against, without giving careful consideration to what the person—in this case, God— had to say. If a person's testimony is valid and therefore reliable, it will be backed up by supporting evidence and will stand up under the closest scrutiny. That is exactly the case with God's Word. Before we get to some of that supporting evidence, I encourage you to be willing to listen to what the Bible says for itself. What we are learning here lifts reading the Bible to a new level. It must be read with an alert mind, a humble heart, and a teachable spirit. If it is the breathed-out word of the Almighty, how else would you read it? Remember, the whole point of the exercise is that God wants to breathe His living Word into you and me through the ministry of the same Holy Spirit who was involved in giving it in the first place.

When we moved into our current home we found a wartime bomb in the basement. To begin with we had fun with it tossing it to one another! We thought it was just a collector's piece which had been left by the previous owners of the house. We decided, however, to have the bomb checked out, only to discover it was live and unexploded. For an entire weekend our house was cordoned off, and a police officer stood guard. Pope John Paul II was in Vancouver so all the bomb disposal units were over there. Eventually some of the bomb squad arrived with a special container and carefully removed our potentially and devastatingly powerful guest! The moment we discovered from the police that the bomb was live, our attitude to it changed radically. Believe me, when we grasp the fact that every word of the Bible, as originally given, is God breathed and, because of that, so dynamically powerful, our attitude to it will also change radically. If only all of us who profess to be followers of Jesus could recapture, and hold forever, the thrill expressed by my granddaughter Riley, when she was given her very first real Bible. Not a chidren's picture version, but a real leather bound one. She was so excited. If only we, in the west, could see, as I have, the sheer joy on the face of one of Jesus persecuted disciples on receiving a copy of God's word. The attitude is one of humble reverence and deepest gratitude. They understand the potential of what they hold in their hands.

It is not too difficult to see now that the Bible, if God-breathed, must be completely authoritative. The stark fact is: God is speaking, so I had better listen and obey. Not with the listening and obedience of a mindless groveller, but with a heart which loves God unconditionally because it is first loved unconditionally by its Creator. Only people who discover or, in some cases, rediscover God's Word, would pump their fist with an excited yes. Why? Because God is breathing His Word into the mind and heart. There is now a two-way communion with God. He is showing me who He is and revealing to me the significance of my Saviour, the Lord Jesus Christ, living inside me by His Holy Spirit. A two-way communion with God can mean finding real answers to the hard questions: "Where did I come from, why am I here, where am I going?"

I will never forget the day I received a phone call in Canada from my dad in Scotland. He had first come to faith in the Lord Jesus Christ as personal Saviour when I was very young. For various reasons, none of them earth shattering, he drifted from his once-vibrant walk with God. In the years leading up to this phone call, I had sensed a mellowing in his heart. The death of a friend seemed to clinch things in his mind, causing him to realize what he had been missing all these years, that he had been in the desert. "I'm just phoning to tell you I have come back to the Lord," he said. I was speechless. I had prayed for this moment for years and now it was a reality. I couldn't believe it. God had answered the prayers of all the years and my immediate reaction was total surprise! How typical is that? It was real, all right. The change in his whole disposition and in his relationship with his wife, my mom, was truly radical. But for me one of the most significant things was his rediscovery of God's Word. Dad was never one for long telephone conversations, but his subsequent calls were no longer taken up with generalities and small talk. He wanted to enthusiastically share what he had been reading in the Word of God. Not only that, but what he and Mom had been reading together.

For many years it has been my privilege to teach in the Capernwray Bible School on Thetis Island in beautiful British Columbia. Brad (not his real name) was typical of some students who attend the school. He was there either because he felt this was the thing for Christian kids in North America to do on graduating from high school or because his parents had insisted he should. My teaching assignment that week was prayer and it happened to come close to the beginning of the school year. As the week began, Brad was obviously not a particularly happy camper. I began to teach that prayer was a crucial part of meaningful reading and understanding of God's Word. As a result of that, Brad suddenly came alive. He came to me later in the week so excited about what God had taught him. "I didn't realize God's Word could be so alive and so exciting," he said. "This is cool!"

It is this living, God-breathed quality that gives the Bible its authority. Failure to realise this will rob the reader of ever discovering how fabulous a real walk with God is. It will also rob the reader of wanting to spend time in God's Word. I will deal with this in more detail later. For now, it needs to be said that reading God's Word as it ought to be read, in dependence on the Holy Spirit, stimulates the mind and creates faith in the reader's heart. This, in turn, leads to a willingness to act obediently on what has been read. The result is continuously fresh growth in the relationship with God.

The Bible Is Totally Unique

The question of the authority of Scripture is very important. So important, in fact, that it stands at the heart of what it means to be a growing Jesus-follower. It makes real the difference between religiosity and relationship with God. As Dr. J. I. Packer puts it when talking about the evangelical view of authority,

> "Its basic principle is that the teaching of the written Scriptures is the Word which God spoke and speaks to His church, and is finally authoritative for faith and life. To learn the mind of God one must consult His written Word."[4]

I mentioned earlier that if an individual's personal testimony is to be proved valid, it must be able to stand up under the closest scrutiny. The Bible's claim is that it is God-breathed. If true, we can look for the stamp of the author on its pages. There are three areas of significance in this connection.

The Harmony of Scripture

First, there is the harmony in Scripture. Josh McDowell points out that the Bible was written over a period of 1,600 years, over 60 generations, by 40 plus authors including kings, peasants, philosophers, fishermen, poets, statesmen, scholars, etc. It was written in many different places like the desert, in a dungeon, in a prison, etc.; in times of peace and war, in joy and despair. It was written on three continents: Asia, Africa, and Europe. It was written in Hebrew, Greek, and Aramaic. It deals with hundreds of controversial subjects and yet the biblical authors spoke about those subjects with complete harmony. Their one harmonious theme from Genesis to Revelation is God's wonderful plan of salvation for mankind through His Son, the Lord Jesus Christ. McDowell says that the chances of such harmony happening, taking only ten authors, from one walk of life, one generation, one place, one time, one mood, one continent, one language on just one controversial subject are nil. He says: "Any man sincerely seeking truth would consider a book with the above uniqueness."[5] No other book in world literature, together with its main character, the historical Jesus, has made and continues to make such an impact on

---

4   J. I. Packer, "Fundamentalism and the Word of God" (I.V.F) 47
5   Josh McDowell, "Evidence that Demands a verdict" (Campus Crusade for Christ)

human history. Bearing this uniqueness in mind, how can you not be thrilled to have a copy in your possession and to make it the foundation of your life and lifestyle?

The Significance of Prophecy

Another area of significance which points to divine authorship is in the area of prophecy. Quite apart from anything else, prophecy by itself is a unique feature of the Bible. It is not something you find in the books of the other world religions. Prophecy, it is estimated, makes up about thirty percent of the content of the Bible. Scholars are in agreement that literally hundreds of Bible prophecies have been fulfilled to the letter. This fact alone is compelling evidence that the Bible has to be taken seriously. I would go as far as to say that the fulfillment of prophecy is one of the greatest encouragements to faith. I quote from evangelist, John Blanchard to illustrate how significant this is. He says:

> "In his book *Science Speaks*, Peter Stoner, Professor Emeritus at Westmont College, California, and charter member of the American Scientific Affiliation, identifies eleven prophecies about Israel taken from the writings of four Old Testament prophets: Isaiah, Jeremiah, Ezekiel and Micah, each of whom claimed to be speaking God's words. These prophecies related to the land as a whole, the destruction of Jerusalem, the rebuilding of the temple and the later enlargement of the city—and every one came true. Calculating the probability of all eleven prophecies being fulfilled by chance to be 8x10 to the power of 63, Stoner then gives an illustration of what this means. He says that if we were to scoop together a pile of coins equal in size to 100 billion stars in each of two trillion galaxies in just one second, add to the pile at the same rate every second, day and night, for twenty-one years, then ask a blindfolded friend to pick out one marked coin

from this incomprehensibly massive pile, his chances of doing so would be the same as the likelihood that these four prophets could have got these things right by guesswork."[6]

Remember, this illustrates only four of the hundreds of fulfilled prophecies in the Bible. Pretty impressive, don't you think?

Professor William Lane Craig says,

"Though many religions boast of revelations showing the way of salvation, only the Scriptures have the support of miracle and prophecy, which prove it to be the true authority."[7]

The Power of the Bible

The third area which demonstrates what could be called the signature of God on His Word is its power to affect the lives of people from every walk of life, from every race and creed, and from every generation. It is very important and encouraging to see that we have very good reasons for faith. Faith is not some leap in the dark or, as the little boy described it, "Believing what you know ain't true." The Word of God is historically reliable, does not contradict science, and is increasingly being demonstrated as archaeologically accurate. Its prophecies have been, are being, and will be fulfilled. But faith is that step beyond reason when the reader of Scripture takes God at His Word and so begins to prove that God cannot be other than totally faithful to His promises. Faith leads to that experiential knowledge of the life-transforming power that is peculiar to the Word of God. This is what the apostle Paul meant when he said, *"I am not ashamed of the gospel for it is the power of God for salvation to everyone who believes"* (Rom. 1:16).

It has been my privilege as an evangelist to be preaching God's Word for many years. Over and over I have seen the life-transforming power of God's Word operating before my eyes in

---

6   John Blanchard, "Is God Past His Sell-By Date?", Evangelical Press, Page 20

7   William Lane Craig, "Reasonable Faith" (Crossway Books)

varied circumstances. While preaching God's Word some years ago, I saw a lady in the congregation with a most skeptical look. Part way through the preaching, her whole expression suddenly changed. Afterwards she told me that was the moment she was born again. An inward transaction took place. Faith took the step beyond mere reason from trusting what she thought she ought to be doing to trusting what Jesus had done for her through His death on the cross. She did not commit intellectual suicide at that moment; she simply took God at His word and acted upon it. A bit like my Aunt Martha did when boarding the plane (see chapter 2). In contrast to that, another individual, on another occasion, angrily challenged me following the preaching of the Word of God: "Who told you I was coming to this event today? Someone must have given you details of my life and circumstances!" No one had. The inherent power in the Word of God was working. That individual went away still angry.

While speaking at Capernwray Hall in England, I was spending time with some young people. I sat with a teenage lad from Germany. He had been listening to the teaching but simply did not see how the Bible could have anything to do with him and his life. He could not understand the meaning of what Jesus had done on the cross. I shared many things with him, praying all the time that the Holy Spirit would open his eyes. Eventually I read Isaiah 53:5 with him: *"But He was pierced through for our transgressions, He was crushed for our iniquities; the chastening for our well-being fell upon Him, and by His scourging we were healed."* His whole expression changed as if someone had switched on a light in his mind. The power in God's Word created faith in his heart.

Their marriage was on the rocks. They could not speak a civil word to one another. In desperation, the young husband phoned and asked me to visit. The atmosphere in the home could almost be cut with a knife. We talked for a while and eventually I advised them to take time to quieten their minds in God's presence. "Go to separate rooms," I said, "and open your Bible and ask God to speak into your situation from His Word. I will see you again in three days." They took my advice and when I returned the atmosphere had changed. The amazing thing was the Holy Spirit had, unknown to them at the time, directed them both to the same verses. The power of God's Word touched their hearts and the marriage was healed because their hearts were healed through responding to the living Word of God. They are still together.

On another occasion, unknown to me, two ladies in the church had a strong disagreement about something. Their relationship as Christians was in ruins for their pride kept them from humbling themselves and apologizing to each other. I was preaching that day from Philippians 4:2: *"I urge Eudia and I urge Syntyche to live in harmony in the Lord."* The power in God's Word broke all barriers. Both women came to me afterwards completely broken. Neither was concerned who was to blame or who started the whole sordid business. What a thrill to see them get themselves right with God and with one another.

The Bible is often dismissed as fallible and unreliable because in the minds of many, it was written by fallible men. That thinking leads to serious questions about why and how certain books came to be included in the Bible. The books included in the Bible are known as the canon of Scripture. The word canon simply means a measuring rod; and as applied to Scripture, came to mean the list of books to be officially accepted as Scripture. In a sense, the same principle applies here as applies to the bodily resurrection of the Lord Jesus from the dead. The early church did not produce this doctrine as part of their belief system. The resurrection became part of the belief system because it had already happened. It was foundational to the life and mission of the early church and is still today. So with the canon of Scripture. Jesus and the apostles believed and taught the Old Testament as the God-breathed Word of God. The apostles received the teaching of Jesus firsthand and made that the basis of what they taught and wrote. Paul described the church as *"God's household, having been built on the foundation of the apostles and prophets, Christ Jesus Himself being the cornerstone"* (Eph. 2:19-20).

The church began to define what was to be included in the

canon of the New Testament about the middle of the second century AD. The criterion used was simply to formally recognize the books which were already recognized as having had the authority of the apostles from day one. Dr. J. I. Packer explains,

> "It seems that the process involved no more than the explicit recognition of an established state of affairs."[8]

The church did not give the books authority; they simply recognized the authority that was already there.

This is significant because it further emphasizes the unique quality of God's Word. This is further reason to ask what place of authority it has when it comes to building our lives and families. Dr. Packer, speaking of the New Testament as "a God-given complement to the Old Testament" says,

> "We should not hesitate to ascribe the process by which [Christianity] sought and found a New Testament to the providential guidance of the Holy Ghost, nor to receive that New Testament as from the hand of Christ, as God-breathed Scripture, inspired and, together with the Old Testament, authoritative for faith and life."[9]

It is helpful to quote McDowell as he gives five guiding principles in determining the books to be included in the canon:

1. Is it authoritative—did it come from the hand of God?

2. Is it prophetic—was it written by a man of God?

3. Is it authentic?—(the fathers had the attitude of 'if in doubt throw it out')

4. Is it dynamic—did it come with the life-transforming power of God?

---

8 J. I. Packer, "Fundamentalism and the Word of God" (I.V.F) 66
9 J. I. Packer, "Fundamentalism and the Word of God" (I.V.F) 67

5. Was it received, collected, read and used—was it accepted by the people of God?[10]

A Challenge

If you claim to be a follower of Jesus, you simply cannot, indeed you must not, become casual in your attitude toward God's Word. Because it is God-breathed, it is the most important, the most valuable, the most dynamic volume you will ever hold. It is God's Word to you, for you to build your life, your family, and your future upon.

> As bread of life, it feeds.
> As wisdom for living, it guides.
> As comfort in hard times, it strengthens.
> As confidence for the future, it encourages.

Something to Ponder

I have often been deeply affected by what the Bible says about the apostle Peter's moment of greatest failure, when he denied that he knew the Lord Jesus: *"Peter was following Him at a distance"* (Matt. 26:58). This was when Jesus was being lied about and falsely accused. Do you ever long to be the person you know God wants you to be in your family and among those you are with every day? As long as you neglect the Word of God and refuse to discipline your life such that you are reading it with a humble, submissive, and obedient heart, you will always remain at a distance, the place of defeat and failure.

---

10 Josh McDowell, "Evidence that Demands a Verdict" (Campus Crusade for Christ) 33f.

FOUR

You Already Hold the Key

Are you filled with the Holy Spirit? Considering what the Bible teaches on the subject, there ought to be no room for uncertainty. Ephesians 5:18 says, *"And do not get drunk with wine, for that is dissipation, but be filled with the Spirit."* As has been pointed out by scholars of the original Bible languages, the grammatical structure of this verse is interesting.

"Be filled" is in the imperative mood. That means it is a command. If I am not filled with the Holy Spirit, I am being disobedient.

It is in the plural form which means it is for every believer. Looking at the context of the verse, no one must be drunk with wine but all must be filled with the Spirit.

It is in the passive voice and could be translated; let the Holy Spirit fill you. He is more willing to fill us than we are to be filled.

It is in the present tense. It is, therefore, meant to be a continuous, ongoing, day-by-day and moment-by-moment experience.

It is worth mentioning that there is no such thing as being drunk with the Holy Spirit or out of control when He fills a life. Remember, the fruit of the Spirit is self-control (Gal. 5:22-23). Dr. John Stott wisely points out,

> "A person who is drunk, we say, is 'under the influence' of alcohol; and certainly a Spirit-filled Christian is under the influence and power of the

Holy Spirit. But there the comparison ends and the contrast begins."[11]

Really Enjoying Your Bible

Think of it! You now hold the key of understanding—the key which opens the door to the rich, thrilling world of God-breathed Scripture. It is a truly life-changing and hope-inspiring world. This is what was at the heart of the teaching of Jesus when He spoke of the Holy Spirit as the Helper. He said, *"He will teach you all things, and bring to your remembrance all that I said to you. He will guide you into all truth. He will glorify Me, for He will take of Mine and will disclose it to you"* (John 14:26; 16:13-14).

I urge you to pause and consider the part the Holy Spirit really plays in your life as a Christian. Ask yourself, right now, if you are filled with the Holy Spirit. In the course of my travels over the years, I have had the privilege of staying with many wonderful Christian families. Almost without exception, when I am welcomed into a home, I am not only made to feel at home but I am told to make myself at home. I know what the good people mean, but I also know serious restrictions go with the generous hospitality. I must never overstep the unspecified, but clearly understood boundaries because I am but a guest. What would you think if your guest began looking through your most personal and private documents or belongings? That changes your guest into an intruder. If you have ever had your home burgled, you know what that feels like! Is your attitude to the Holy Spirit like that? You're glad He is in your life but you know and He knows there are serious boundaries, even though you profess to want to be filled with the Holy Spirit. Perhaps you look on the Holy Spirit as a bit of an intruder when He wants to look into the personal and intimate areas of your life. That is the essence of being filled. No restrictions, no intimate area closed, but a total abandonment of every part of your life to the presence of God.

This is important because it is precisely what Scripture means when it talks of a life being filled with God's presence.

---

11   John R.W. Stott, "God's New Society" (I.V.P) 204

In Paul's great prayer for the Christians at Ephesus, he prays that they would be *"strengthened with power through His Spirit in the inner man, so that Christ may dwell in your hearts through faith that you may be filled up to all the fullness of God"* (Eph. 3:14-21). To dwell means to be there as a resident in His own home, not as a lodger or a guest. This is why Jesus has to do a deep work in many of us. We must come to a willingness to surrender everything. Jesus must reign with total authority over our most personal and intimate areas. In the safety deposit box of your life, what do you keep locked away from Jesus? The expression—the presence of God; His light, purity, love, freedom, joy, peace, and hope—will only be real as we surrender so He can fill us with Himself. All those things are who Jesus is. Where He is, they are also. It is absolutely mind-boggling to think this is what God wants for us as His children. The important thing to see is that He can't lead us into the riches of His Word under any other circumstances. Where Jesus is Lord, the Holy Spirit fills the life, the power of God flows, the passion for God's Word grows and its vast treasures are opened up. I encourage you to stop, take some quiet time to think, and pray through the implications of what you just read. It could be the most important thing you will ever do in your Christian life. You may have all the principles of biblical interpretation (hermeneutics) and all the required tools at your fingertips. You may be proficient in both the original languages, Hebrew and Greek. All of these are helpful and desirable, but apart from being filled with the Holy Spirit—having Christ reigning in your life—your reading and study of the Bible will never go beyond being merely an academic exercise. It is meant to be deeply satisfying, a meeting with God, feeding on the most nourishing of food and drinking from the most refreshing stream. There ought to be the sense of inner rest and quietness coming from being focused on Jesus and not on self. All this and the awareness of being given wisdom and direction in coping with the good times and the bad times in life makes the regular meeting with God in His Word something to be eagerly looked forward to.

Interpreting God's Word

That's just your interpretation! How often have you heard that when you have tried to share what the Bible says on some important issue? Let's be honest here, sometimes Christians are guilty of developing the weirdest ideas in their reading and interpretation of the Word of God. Yes, we do have the Holy Spirit but we are still imperfect. One of the key issues is the reader's attitude. It must be one of humility and having a teachable spirit. That is why, among the gifts given to the church by the Lord, there are *"pastors and teachers, for the equipping of the saints for the work of service"* (Eph. 4:11-12).

To arrive at a balanced and godly interpretation of any part of God's Word, there are clear guidelines which are reliable, honest, and intellectually satisfying. They take into account that it is reasonable to expect God's Holy Spirit, who inspired Scripture, to be involved in its interpretation. Using these principles will make your reading and study of God's Word so much more fulfilling and will give you a greater sense that you really are living in a healthy relationship with the Lord. It will be challenging because sometimes long-held pet theories will have to be abandoned. Having to ask if a view you held is truly biblical can be humbling. That is not a bad thing; the less there is of you and me in the matter, the better things will be for everyone. Walking in fellowship with God and with His people is all that matters.

I was given some advice I have never forgotten: that if anything I think I'm experiencing from God does not produce greater humility, it is a false and self-centred experience. True biblical understanding will always result in less of me, and more of Jesus being evident.

There are certain foundational doctrines of the faith which are not up for discussion—non-negotiables—doctrines like the inspiration of Scripture, the deity of the Lord Jesus, the virgin birth of Christ, His sinless life, His atoning death and bodily resurrection, the Holy Spirit, and the second advent of the Lord Jesus. Outside of these foundational doctrines, there are grey areas about which the best and godliest of scholars do not always see eye to eye. That is why I am saying all of us must approach

God's Word with a humble and teachable spirit. A grey area for some may not seem so grey for others. No matter what the shade of grey, such matters need not affect your basic relationship with God. It could, however, affect the enjoyment of that relationship, especially if you allow hanging on to your grey area, no matter what, to make you over-dogmatic. Such an attitude leads to pride and maybe even anger and a bitter spirit.

Here are the helpful principles alluded to earlier for understanding God's Word. In these next few paragraphs I am drawing heavily from Dr. Bruce Milne.[12]

The Bible is infallible as correctly interpreted. We can identify four major principles.

Scripture must be interpreted literally

This principle, technically known as the historico-grammatical method, takes the natural, straightforward sense of a text or passage as fundamental. This "literal" approach must be carefully distinguished from the "literalistic." The latter interprets the words of scripture in a wooden fashion without making allowance for imagery, metaphor, literary form, etc.

A "literal" approach requires that we interpret scripture:

- According to the original meaning. God's Word is almost always immediately relevant to the situation to which it was addressed.
- According to literary form. The Bible is made up of all kinds of literature: poetry, prose, parables, allegory (Ezek. 16), apocalyptic (Rev.), fable (Judg. 9: 8-15), etc.
- According to context.

Scripture must be interpreted by Scripture

This principle recognizes the unity and self-consistency of Scripture, deriving from its single divine author.

Interpret according to the purpose of Scripture (John 20:31;

---

12 Bruce Milne, "Know the Truth - A Handbook of Christian Belief" (Inter Varsity Press), 45-47.

2 Tim. 3:15). It is given to make us "wise for salvation."

Interpret in the light of other passages on the same theme.

Interpret the earlier in the light of the later and fuller. In particular, the New Testament interprets the Old Testament.

Scripture can be interpreted only by the Holy Spirit

This neither absolves us from hard work, nor implies that we can isolate ourselves from other Christians in our understanding of the Bible. God's Spirit is holy; therefore, what we understand of His truth is related less to the capacity of our brains than to the extent of our obedience.

Scripture must be interpreted dynamically

What does it mean for today in my life? Reading God's Word has the potential of becoming for you the most important, life-transforming activity you will ever undertake. More will be said later about how to make the most of it but for now, ask yourself some simple questions each time you read a passage of Scripture:

What does it say? In other words, read it carefully. I will never forget pontificating to my father-in-law about what I thought a particular passage meant. He listened quietly and graciously then simply said, "Clayton, read it again!" Thankfully I did. Through a more careful reading, it dawned on me that it simply did not say what I had thought. I learned a huge lesson.

What does it mean? Be prepared to dig deeper by doing your own research. Read the passage in several of the translations available today. I will say more about study tools later.

What does it teach? Your reading of God's Word must be done in a prayerful attitude. The Holy Spirit will teach you as you faithfully apply yourself to your Bible. There is nothing more exciting than having your eyes opened so what God is really saying through some passage of His Word dawns upon your understanding. This must be accompanied by an attitude of willing obedience. Seeing something God wants you to do and then refusing to do it is a recipe for stopping your growth as a Christian.

Taking wise counsel from a more mature fellow-Christian, who is more grounded in God's Word than you, will be an enormous help in avoiding pitfalls and unhelpful tangents.

A Challenge

Have you been neglecting God's Word? Do you feel you have to apologize to God for your attitude to this amazing and unique treasure He has given you?

Something to Ponder

Could it be that you have become over-dogmatic on some grey area of scriptural teaching? Has this resulted in a bad spirit on your part that has spoiled your fellowship with some of your brothers and sisters in Christ? Perhaps it's time to humble yourself and repent.

FIVE

Moving On in Faith

Knowing what we now know about the Bible—its uniqueness, its authority, its power—there is nothing else to be done other than moving on in faith. It should be clear by now that there are good reasons for faith. I am not talking about a leap in the dark, but about faith that moves forward with confidence. *"Now faith is the assurance* [literally, that which gives substance to] *of things hoped for, the conviction* [literally the proving by testing] *of things not seen"* (Heb. 11:1). This is faith that makes a choice and says, "I choose to take God at His word." May I say with great conviction that until you get there, the Bible will never consistently be *"the Word of God* [which] *is living and active"* (Heb. 4:12) in your life. What reading of it you do will either be nothing more than an academic exercise or a chore to be over with as quickly as possible—your spiritual exercise for the day. You may feel better having done it but only on the level of how you feel when you clean your teeth.

There are many professing Christians who still have a problem accepting the Bible as the living Word of the living God from beginning to end. Believe me, such people do nothing to enhance their academic status by taking such an attitude. The Bible is historically, scientifically, and archaeologically accurate and reliable from Genesis to Revelation. You can only contrast it with but never compare it to other religious books. It stands totally separate and absolutely unique. The bottom line is a matter of choice, a matter of the will. Are you or are you not going to take God at His word and move forward in faith? Make no mistake; you most certainly will begin to move forward, to grow and, best of all, to become more like Jesus.

To illustrate the importance of this, see Colossians 3:15-16. Verse 15 says, *"Let the peace of Christ rule* (literally, be the umpire, the deciding factor) *in your hearts to which indeed you were called in one body; and be thankful."* Where do you think this peace, this ability to make good and wise decisions for yourself, your family, and your pathway through life, comes from? See verse 16. *"Let the word of Christ richly dwell within you with all wisdom."*

This does not mean you use the Bible in an almost superstitious way. Ephesians 5:17 says, *"So then do not be foolish, but understand what the will of the Lord is."* Dr. John Stott, commenting on this verse says,

> "[God's] 'general' will is found in Scripture; the will of God for the people of God has been revealed in the Word of God. But we shall not find His 'particular' will in Scripture. To be sure, we shall find general principles in Scripture to guide us, but detailed decisions have to be made after careful thought and prayer and the seeking of advice from mature and experienced believers."[13]

Many great minds have wrestled with what the correct attitude to the Bible ought to be. Many have questioned its inspiration and, consequently, its authority. At the end of the day, I believe it is true to say that, for great minds and for lesser minds, the matter is settled on the choice whether to believe God or not. The human mind can grapple with the inspiration and the authority of Scripture, but it is only faith that can bring the person behind the mind into the experience of Scripture's living, life-changing power.

In his autobiography, Dr. Billy Graham tells of his struggles in this area.

> "The particular intellectual problem I was wrestling with, for the first time since my conversion

---

13   John R.W. Stott, God's New Society" (I.V.P) 203

as a teenager, was the inspiration and authority of the Scriptures. Could the Bible be trusted completely? I was the president of a liberal arts college, Bible school, and seminary—an institution whose doctrinal statement was extremely strong and clear on this point."

By this time Dr. Graham was thirty; his struggle became so intense he says, "I had to have an answer. If I could not trust the Bible, I could not go on." One night while walking in the moonlight, he placed his open Bible on a tree stump.

"The exact wording of my prayer is beyond recall but it must have echoed my thoughts: 'O God! There are many things in this book I do not understand. There are many problems with it for which I have no solution. There are many seeming contradictions. There are some areas in it which do not seem to correlate with modern science. I can't answer some of the philosophical and psychological questions.'

He went on to say,

"I was trying to be on the level with God, but something remained unspoken. At last the Holy Spirit freed me to say it. 'Father I am going to accept this as Thy Word—by faith! I'm going to allow faith to go beyond my intellectual questions and doubts, and I will believe this to be Your inspired Word.' When I got up from my knees I sensed the presence of God as I had not sensed it in months. Not all my questions had been answered, but a major bridge had been crossed. In my heart and mind, I knew a spiritual battle in my soul had been fought and won."[14]

It is very interesting to note that the next thing in Dr. Graham's schedule following that prayer of faith was the great Los Angeles campaign of 1949. This turned out to be the turning

---

14   Billy Graham, "Just As I Am" (Harper Collins) 137- 140

point in the ministry of God's servant, the event that launched Billy Graham onto the world stage as a faithful evangelist.

Sometimes people say to me, "I wish I had faith like so and so." What they don't realize is that if they would only get into the Word of God, really seeking God in the process, faith will be created in their hearts. It is as the Bible says, *"So faith comes from hearing, and hearing by the word of Christ"* (Rom. 10:17).

Among Christians, nothing grieves God's Holy Spirit so much as the sin of unbelief (not taking God at His word). It grieves Him because when we refuse to believe, and thus do not take God at His word, we forfeit the rich experience of proving what God is longing to do for us. I encourage you to read Hebrews 11, the great chapter about faith. Having given us the definition of faith in the first verse, the writer makes this powerful statement in verse 6, *"And without faith it is impossible to please Him, for he who comes to God must believe that He is and that He is the rewarder of those who seek Him."* In Hebrews 3:12, there is a clear warning about the dangers of *"an evil unbelieving heart that falls away from the living God."* This verse shows that this particular sin is at the heart of all spiritual decline in the lives of so many of God's people. It's what robs so many of their joy in Christ, their victory over sin, and their desire to share their faith with others. It is at the heart of all that is involved in our relationship with the living God. Any professing Christian who is not operating in faith is not growing because they are not allowing the Holy Spirit who lives inside them to do in them and through them the kind of things only He can do. We simply have to get this right if we really want to discover all that God has for us in our relationship with Him.

Learning to Prioritize

It's true, the battle is won in the area of faith and faith is a choice, an act of the will. Having won that battle, the next area of challenge is with time and priorities. Now that you have determined to move on in faith, you will be motivated by a far greater sense of purpose. You will soon realize what countless generations of Christians before you have come to realize: the devil's greatest and most concentrated area of activity is to keep you from the prayerful reading and study of God's Word. This is at the heart of so much of the weakness and defeat in individual Christians and in churches.

When speaking at a conference, I had been dealing with the theme of listening to God by spending time in His Word. As people were preparing to go home, a lady told me God had challenged her deeply about the lack of time she had given to reading her Bible. So much so that she and a friend had covenanted to keep one another accountable and so encourage one another in this area. I'll never forget her words as she stated what her previous attitude had been, because they perfectly sum up this debilitating disease that is afflicting the church in the twenty-first century: "Lord, I'm glad you are in my life as my Saviour, but I'm sorry, I just don't have time for your Word."

Would that more of us were that honest. God deeply convicted me of this many years ago. This is a battle that must be won. Being a loser here always results in weakness and defeat. Unless you win this battle, you will never be able to worship or be a true worship leader, no matter how gifted you may be. You will never be the parent God means you to be. You will never be an effective church leader.

I humbly submit that too many pastors and preachers are losing this battle. They have allowed themselves to be so caught up with administration and people stuff, they do not give adequate time to new and fresh study projects out of which would come new and fresh preaching material. They are not preaching the Word; this is why their people are not being fed. The only thing that will feed the people of God is the Word of God. If the preacher is not constantly being nourished by the fresh study of God's Word, his people will not be nourished.

One of my closest friends is a faithful pastor. God challenged him deeply about the lack of time he was giving to the prayerful study of the Word. He told his congregation one Sunday that from then on he would be giving less time to administration and to other demands and far more time to the prayerful study of God's Word. The people gave him a standing ovation.

If you are reading this as a pastor, may I remind you that your people come to hear from God, not you. They come every Sunday, battered by all that the godless world can throw at them, hungry for the nourishing food that can only be found in the Word of God. Study the Word for all you are worth; out of what God gives you will come His Word for His people—real food for the hungry sheep.

How do we get this right? Please understand, you have a choice in the matter. Every area of life is involved. What kind of memories do you want your children to have of you as a parent? Dr. James Dobson of Focus on the Family said, "The only thing you will take with you into eternity is your children." What taste do you want to leave in the mouths of your work colleagues when it comes to matters of integrity? Too often it has been said, "If that's what a Christian looks like, I don't want to be one." If you ever move house, what would your old neighbours say about you to the people who move in? Would it be, "They were moody and unhelpful but very religious"? If your doctor says you are terminally ill, what would you do with your mind and heart to cope? When serious persecution comes to your country, will you be prepared to stand firm?

These and many other questions deal with the really important issues of life and death. Far more important than career advancement or wealth and possessions. How you or I answer those questions is directly related to the place the Word of God has in our lives. We must be willing to move forward in faith. We must be willing to believe God. We must trust His Word as inspired and infallible as originally given. We must see it as finally authoritative for all matters of life and death. Otherwise we will never be able to cope with life's real issues, with the victory and dignity God intended.

The late Dr. Keith Price, minister at large with the Evangelical Fellowship of Canada and for many years a close friend, was given the news he had cancer. He told his children, "Up till now I have tried to teach you how to live; now I want to teach you how to die."[15] And he did, with victory and great dignity. He

---

15   Keith Price *"Thirsting After God"* (Christian Publications Inc)

was a man with a passion for God and His Word.

What we are talking about here applies to what Stephen Covey calls private victory. He is dealing with what he calls "the seven habits of highly effective people."[16] The first three of the seven habits are in the area of the private life:

- Be pro-active.
- Begin with the end in mind.
- Put first things first.

In our walk with God these three habits are very applicable. When talking about being pro-active, Covey says you have a "response ability—the ability to choose your response." In other words, just get on with it and stop making excuses.

For the Jesus-follower, having the end in mind goes far beyond worldly success to being a godly success as a parent, child, employer, employee, elder, pastor, etc. That means looking forward with anticipation to standing at the judgment seat of Christ (Rom. 14:10) where rewards for faithfulness will be given. That means being rewarded by the Lord Jesus Himself for being faithful wherever God has placed you in life.

Putting first things first involves majoring on what is really important. Covey points out in his book how most of us never win the battle of the urgent against the important. Too often it is the urgent that wins—all the things on that to-do list. We never seem to get to what is really important. If you stop to think about it, the important is what your heart longs to do.

Why not make up your mind before God to do it? The Bible teaches that, at the end of the day, what God is interested in is our heart motivation. Be encouraged by that. God knows that, as you read this book, your heart motivation is to move forward in faith. He gave you that motivation because He, at this moment, is living inside you by His Holy Spirit. Yield to His prompting now and make whatever changes need to be made in your lifestyle so you make the time for God's Word.

---

16 Stephen Covey, *"The Seven Habits of Highly Effective People"* (Simon and Schuster)

Develop Good Habits

When I was a young bank employee, I wanted so badly to be faithful in my witness in the office. There were many times I failed, but I thank God for the things He taught me then. I knew I had to spend time in God's Word, otherwise I would fail even more than I did. Also, I would not even want to be a faithful witness in the office if God's Word was not fresh in my heart each day. The evenings were hopeless for me because I had to either attend evening classes or study in preparation for writing bank exams. It had to be in the early morning before I left for work. To be sure I got up, I put the alarm clock far from the bed so I had to get up to turn it off! I didn't want to incur the wrath of the rest of the family by waking them if the alarm kept ringing! Those early morning sessions laid important foundations.

During the first few days of my student years in Bible school, we had a lecture from College Principal Rev. Andrew McBeath, one of the saintliest men it has been my privilege to know. Like Zaccheus, being small in stature, he was affectionately known in that Scottish bastion of theology as the wee man! Mr. McBeath was talking to the student body about personal discipline, especially in the area of quiet time in God's Word every day. He said that, in the busyness of college life, if we did not make time early in the day for God's Word and prayer, it was likely the time with God would not happen. I'll never forget his response when someone asked, "How do you get up early in the morning?" "Oh," he said in his quiet way, "you just get up."

That's it! More Christians need to adopt the Nike slogan and "just do it." Good habits, and there is none better than the daily practice of spending quiet time with God and His Word, are matters of personal discipline. Be hard on yourself. It won't do you any harm. It will do you a world of good. There is not going to be one meaningful moment spent in God's Word that you will ever regret. If you are a young person, there will never be a better time than now to establish the good habits involved in developing your walk with God. The older you get, the harder it becomes. How many regrets are there in the lives of those of us who are older that go back to allowing bad habits to form?

Maybe you are genuinely not a morning person. I believe morning is the best time to be alone with God because that is when there are the fewest distractions. It could be, however, that the best time for you is later in the day or when circumstances allow. Make that your time with God.

Something to Ponder

Is the urgent always winning over the important in your life? It does not have to be that way. What are you going to do about it?

SIX

Absolutely Not to Be Missed

One of my closest friends, Bill Innes, passed away having lived a very full and effective life as a follower of Jesus. As a man of integrity in business, as a husband, father, and grandfather, he was a wonderful example. Bill began life, having been abandoned as a newborn on a doorstep wrapped in a newspaper. He grew up in a children's home, completed his education, and went into the fire service. He rose to the position of deputy fire chief at a huge oil refinery. At one stage in his career, Bill turned down the position of fire chief because he felt the added responsibility would interfere with his life and commitments as a disciple of the Lord Jesus. It is very rare to meet someone like Bill, who, in spite of his difficult start in life, was so grateful to God for all that had come his way because he had come to know the Lord Jesus as personal Saviour and Lord.

Bill has always been an inspiration to me and I tell you part of his story, hoping he will be to you too. Would you be willing to make that kind of sacrifice so nothing would stand in the way of your progress as a follower of Jesus? Your challenges may well be different from Bill's but the principle applies. It is vitally important to remember what being a real Christian means. We are not talking about what religion you belong to, we are dealing with the quality of life we could and should be living as people created in God's image. Where we are going to spend eternity when this short life is over is the bottom line. We must take time to be sure we are clear about such things. To become a real Christian in the first place involves a realization of our desperate plight if we have never been born again, to use the Bible term (John 3:7). This is something Jesus said must happen because there is no other way to belong to God's kingdom. The whole point of Jesus' coming into the world was to bring the kingdom of God to the world. Just prior to His crucifixion, when Jesus was on trial before Pilate, He said, *"My kingdom is not of this world"* (John 18:36). In Luke 10, Jesus said that if people rejected His message which was being preached by His representatives, they were rejecting His kingdom. That is a truly serious situation to be in because it means being in the kingdom of this world. God's Word makes it clear that *"the whole world lies in the power of the evil one"* (1 Jn. 5:19). It means to be in the kingdom of Satan. To reject the message of the kingdom of God is to take sides with the kingdom which lies in the power of the evil one. God's judgement in hell has been prepared for the devil and his angels (Matt. 25:41). Clearly, to reject the message of the kingdom of God is to suffer the same judgment as the one in whose kingdom you choose to be.

Some people find these things offensive. Yet they are part of the God-breathed Scripture. We must pay attention to what God has to say. If the idea of God's judgment is not true, what would be the point of the crucifixion of the Lord Jesus Christ? There would be no meaning to the words, *"But God demonstrates His own love toward us, in that while we were yet sinners, Christ died for us"* (Rom. 5:8). Sinners describes those who rebel against God, like the devil to whose kingdom they belong. It's a word which describes the condition of every human being, inherited from the previous generations right back to Adam and Eve in the Garden of Eden. The rebellious Satan tempted them to join him in his rebellion and, because they agreed, every generation since has inherited that sinful nature. Those of us who are parents know that training our children is always in the area of what is good. Their lying, cheating, and temper tantrums come naturally.

At this stage, we need to take time to bring this into the realm of everyday experience. As I write, I am going through some health challenges. The problem of suffering is huge. Reconciling the presence of suffering with the idea of a loving God is difficult for so many people. I have found it helpful to remember that while, as a Jesus-follower, I am part of the kingdom of God, I am still living in the domain of Satan's kingdom. I can't avoid being affected by all that is around me in a world that has rebelled against God. This world, as a result of its rebellion, is suffering the inevitable consequences of the presence of evil. My body is mortal because *"through one man sin entered into the world, and death through sin, and so death spread to all men, because all sinned"* (Rom. 5:12).

The difference made by being a Jesus-follower and therefore, part of God's kingdom, is that Jesus reigns as King in my life. He lives in me by the Holy Spirit. Therefore, as I live in the domain of Satan's kingdom (this world), I live in the power of the kingdom of God which is inside me. I may have all kinds of challenges to face, but my relationship with King Jesus is what brings the amazing peace, and even joy, through it all. There is a wonderful illustration of this in 2 Corinthians chapter 4. Paul is speaking about the gospel as a treasure in earthen vessels. He explains the difference made as the Jesus-follower lives this temporary existence: *"But we have this treasure in earthen vessels, so that the surpassing greatness of the power will be of God and not from ourselves; we are afflicted in every way, but not crushed; perplexed, but not despairing; persecuted, but not forsaken; struck down, but not destroyed so that the life of Jesus also may be manifested in our mortal flesh"* (vv. 7–11).

While in the midst of my health challenges, I was told that the seriousness of the situation would mean some radical lifestyle changes. This is when it all matters. The relevance of the God-breathed Scripture, together with the reality of the Holy Spirit living inside me, brought such peace and joy. I was not happy with my circumstances, but my joy was real. It was my birthday and I was reading Jeremiah, chapters 17 and 18. In chapter 17 I read, *"Blessed is the man who trusts in the Lord and whose trust is the Lord. For he will be like a tree planted by the water, that extends its roots by a stream and will not fear when the heat comes; but its leaves will be green and it will not be anxious in a year of drought nor cease to yield fruit"* (vv. 7–8). In chapter 18 I read about being like clay in the hands of the potter. A birthday card came that day from my dear friends, David and Beryl. They shared the same verses from

Jeremiah 17. It was like a gentle whisper from the Holy Spirit, bringing the peace of God. There is absolutely nothing to compare with standing by faith on the great God-breathed promises of the Bible. That is when we allow the Holy Spirit to make the life of Jesus so real.

As far as the general population of the world is concerned, the devil's greatest concentration of effort is in keeping them in his godless kingdom by veiling their minds so they will not see what God has to offer. God's Word tells us, *"And even if our gospel is veiled, it is veiled to those who are perishing, in whose case the god of this world has blinded the minds of the unbelieving so that they might not see the light of the gospel of the glory of Christ, who is the image of God"* (2 Cor. 4:3-4).

What Does God have to offer

All this raises the question: what does God have to offer? It is absolutely mind-boggling.

Unconditional love: *"In this is love, not that we loved God, but that He loved us and sent His Son to be the propitiation* [literally, the atoning sacrifice] *for our sins"* (1 Jn. 4:10).

Limitless grace: (the grace of God is His giving us what we do not deserve): *"For by grace you have been saved through faith; and that not of yourselves, it is the gift of God; not as a result of works so that no one can boast"* (Eph. 2:8-9).

Rich mercy: (God's mercy is Him not giving us what we do deserve). *"We were by nature children of wrath, even as the rest. But God, being rich in mercy, because of His great love with which He loved us, even when we were dead in our transgressions, made us alive together with Christ* (by grace you have been saved) *and raised us up with Him, and seated us with Him in the heavenly places in Christ Jesus"* (Eph. 2:3-5).

Complete forgiveness: *"In Him we have redemption through His blood, the forgiveness of our trespasses, according to the riches of His grace"* (Eph. 1:7).

Removal of guilt: *"How much more will the blood of Christ, who through the eternal Spirit, offered Himself without blemish to*

God, cleanse your conscience from dead works to serve the living God?" (Heb. 9:14).

No record kept of past sins: *"For I will be merciful to their iniquities, and I will remember their sins no more"* (Heb. 8:12).

Power to live a holy and victorious life: *"I have been crucified with Christ; and it is no longer I who live, but Christ lives in me; and the life which I now live in the flesh I live by faith in the Son of God, who loved me and gave Himself up for me"* (Gal. 2:20).

Somewhere to belong: *"And if one member suffers, all the members suffer with it; if one member is honoured, all the members rejoice with it. Now you are Christ's body, and individually members of it"* (1 Cor. 12:26-27).

Hope for the future: *"Blessed be the God and Father of our Lord Jesus Christ, who according to His great mercy has caused us to be born again to a living hope through the resurrection of Jesus Christ from the dead, to obtain an inheritance which is imperishable and undefiled and will not fade away, reserved in heaven for you, who are protected by the power of God through faith for a salvation ready to be revealed in the last time"* (1 Pet. 1:3-5).

To enjoy those nine things experientially, a radical transaction must take place. The Bible talks about it, as we saw in the reference to Galatians 2:20 above, in terms of Christ living in the individual. In John 3, Jesus said it was literally being born again. Paul taught that it meant becoming a new creature in Christ (2 Cor. 5:17). Religiosity (attending church regularly, being involved in lots of good activities, etc.) and truly being reconciled to God, completely part company. Jesus taught us that it is possible to prophesy in His name, and in His name cast out demons, and in His name perform many miracles and still end up in hell (Matt. 7:15-23). What Jesus wants us to grasp is that we must stop thinking in terms of doing; being is all that matters. It is a question of being born again, of being a new creature, of being something it is impossible to be apart from a miracle of God's grace. The doing follows. When talking about being saved by the grace of God, the Bible makes it clear that when that has happened *"we are His workmanship, created in Christ Jesus for good works, which God prepared beforehand so that we would walk in them"* (Eph. 2:10).

If you read Ephesians 2:8-10 carefully, you will see that no amount of doing on our part will cut it with God when it comes to the matter of becoming someone who is His workmanship. As we have seen, the meaning of God's grace is that He is giving us, as a gift, something we do not deserve. To try to work for what is the gift of His grace, namely becoming His workmanship, is a contradiction. The point is: we cannot work to become what only God can make us. The emphasis has to be moved from our doing, to what God has done. That brings us to the heart of it all—the death that Jesus died on the cross on our behalf. When that happened, He did all the doing that needed to be done. Our part? Simply accept it and make it the focus of our faith. Stop trying to do and simply trust what has been done. What has been done is totally sufficient.

Second Corinthians 5 talks about becoming a new creature (2 Cor. 5:17); the context deals with persuading people to be reconciled to God. Paul, in that reconciling ministry, tells us the controlling factor in it all is the love of Christ. He says, *"having concluded this, that one died for all, therefore all died"* (v. 14). As Prof. James Denney pointed out, Paul is telling us that Jesus died the death we ought to have died: "It was the death of all men which was died by Him."[17] He was our substitute, taking the judgment of God for our sin upon Himself. He did for us what we simply could never do for ourselves. It is really an insult to God to argue with this. There is absolutely no virtue in thinking there must be something we can do. Transferring from the kingdom of Satan to the kingdom of God is completely beyond the power of sinful people like us. It is beyond our power because it means literally being made someone completely new on the inside which is the result of being reconciled to God.

What is involved in transferring from the kingdom of Satan to the kingdom of God? Remember, the Bible describes what is taking place (being born again and becoming a new creature in Christ); that can't happen without our beginning a process of changing radically and growing in holiness. Such a person has to become aware that the transaction which has taken place is

---

17   Prof. James Denney, "The Death of Christ" 84

truly life changing. It is literally a change from darkness to light and from the dominion of Satan to God (Acts 26:18). It is very important to understand how this change happens. Otherwise, it won't work and the Bible will forever remain a dead book.

First, we must understand that Jesus' death on the cross as our substitute is central to everything. The cross stands between the two kingdoms. This is clearly expressed by Paul in Galatians 6:14: *"May it never be that I would boast, except in the cross of our Lord Jesus Christ, through which the world is crucified to me, and I to the world."* Meaning? That when we come to the cross, realizing Jesus did all that needs to be done for our salvation and we trust Him by turning our lives over to Him as personal Saviour and Lord, the transaction takes place. The cross is a bridge from one kingdom to the other. The kingdom of this sinful world, which is under Satan (1 Jn. 5:19), is left behind and we begin to live in the kingdom of God. When you become a Christian, a Jesus-follower, your life comes under new management. A new king rules over your life. The cross, once a bridge, now stands as a separator, between you and this sinful world. You will still live a responsible and productive life, but you need to realize that becoming a Jesus-follower means the world system is finished with us and we with it. You are a new creation. Jesus Christ lives inside you by the Holy Spirit. Every part of your life—personal, family, business, finances—is submitted to His authority and will. The difference this makes is the difference between darkness and light. The nine items mentioned previously now become reality. Life has new meaning and purpose. The presence of God becomes real, no matter how bad things get. The future is filled with hope.

This helps us understand why so many people say it is impossible to live up to the standard Jesus set in the Sermon on the Mount (Matt. 5–7). Of course, it is impossible! That is the whole point. We can only live in the kingdom of God by the power of God. When Jesus lives His life inside you and me, the things we consider humanly impossible become divinely possible. It is a question of allowing Jesus to reproduce His life in us and through us.

How can you be sure you have truly taken this vital step of faith? There is no doubt that by taking this step of faith you are about to embark on a truly life-changing transaction. You must understand what the God-breathed instructions are. The teaching of Acts 2:38 is so clear. Peter had just preached his great sermon on the day of Pentecost, the day the Holy Spirit came to take the place of Jesus on earth. When his listeners heard him, they wanted to know what to do next. Here are Peter's clear instructions: *"Repent, and each of you be baptized in the name of Jesus Christ for the forgiveness of your sins; and you will receive the gift of the Holy Spirit"* (Acts 2:38). Let's unpack this. To repent means to change your mind about your sinfulness. Acknowledge that your inherited sinful nature, which expresses itself in wrong actions, puts you in a position of complete separation from God in Satan's kingdom. Genuine repentance means you will want, more than anything, to turn your back on Satan's kingdom and all that it represents and move into God's kingdom. This is why the Bible uses such expressions as turning from darkness to light, born again, a new creature, etc. It is that radical.

Next, "be baptised in the name of Jesus Christ." Baptism demonstrates how real a person's repentance has been. Being immersed in water is a picture of Jesus going into the grave, having died for the sin of the world. When you are baptized you are saying, *"Jesus' death was for me. I am being baptized into His death"* (Rom. 6:3). This signifies that you have identified yourself with Him. You can say, "He is my Saviour, the One I'm trusting." Coming out of the water is a picture of Jesus rising from the dead, triumphant over death and so, over sin, Satan, and his evil kingdom. Being baptized means giving public expression to the great transaction that took place in your life: you repented, you turned your back on sin, Satan, his kingdom, and everything to do with it. You are now free from Satan's kingdom and in the kingdom of God. You have used the cross as a bridge to move from one kingdom to another. You are a new person living a new life. Romans 6 continues the picture in verses 4:

> "Therefore we have been buried with Him through
> baptism into death, so that as Christ was raised

from the dead through the glory of the Father, so
we too might walk in newness of life."

Baptism is a public expression of what has happened in your
life. Its being public is important. Jesus talked about confessing
Him before men. Baptism is saying, "I'm finished with Satan's
kingdom and everything to do with it and I'm living my life in
the kingdom of God. My family, friends, and people who know
me can expect to see a radical change. My life and lifestyle are
now ruled by Jesus; I belong to His kingdom."

I heard an amusing story about a new Christian who was
baptized. After his baptism, a tobacco pipe was found floating
in the water. When asked about it, he said the pipe did not belong to him anymore but to the old life which he had left behind. He understood the significance of his baptism!

If a person is not prepared to go public with his or her repentance and faith in Christ, serious questions have to be asked
as to whether that repentance and faith are real. Baptism is the
vehicle God has chosen to give expression to the most radical
and far-reaching transaction that can take place in anyone's life.
If you have been set free from Satan's kingdom, from its darkness, lostness, and hopelessness, why would you not want to
go public? You will want the world to know and to share what
you have found.

Real repentance and faith are for the forgiveness of your
sins; and [so that] you will receive the gift of the Holy Spirit. Here is the key to living in the kingdom of God. You now
have the Lord Jesus living His life inside you by the Holy Spirit.
Whatever your past in Satan's kingdom might have involved, it
is gone forever—no more guilt, fear, defeat, or lostness. You are
in a position to appreciate and enjoy:

- unconditional love
- limitless grace
- rich mercy
- complete forgiveness
- removal of guilt
- no record of past sins

- power to live a holy and victorious life
- somewhere to belong
- hope for the future

It simply does not get any better than that.

Something to Ponder

Are you in God's kingdom? If not, you can be. Would you like to be? If so, just talk to God in this suggested prayer:

> Lord, I realize that I'm not in Your kingdom. I'm still in Satan's kingdom, in the lostness and hopelessness of my sin. By faith I turn my back on everything to do with Satan's kingdom (my sin, and consequent lostness and hopelessness).
>
> I repent now and turn to You, Lord Jesus. I choose to trust You and You only as my personal Saviour and Lord. I choose to trust what You have done for me through Your death and resurrection, realizing it is a matter of what You have done for me and not what I can do for myself. I can do nothing to take myself out of Satan's kingdom into Your kingdom.
>
> Please forgive all my sin and wrongdoing. I open my whole life to You. Please come and live in my life as my Saviour and my Lord. Please fill me with Your Holy Spirit and live Your life in me and through me from this moment on.
>
> Thank You for hearing and answering my prayer. Thank You for giving me Your gift of eternal life. I am willing to tell my family and friends I have given my life to You and I'm willing to show them I mean this by being baptized and becoming active in the fellowship of Your people in a church. Amen.

SEVEN

But Life Is So Demanding

We have come to the place of recognizing that being a real Christian involves a radical lifestyle change. That means no matter how demanding life is, and it is pretty demanding, everything is seen through different eyes. Jesus is now Lord and that means seeing everything in the light of God's Word. Scripture is now the roadmap for life. Bearing in mind what has already been said about how we ought to interpret God's Word, the real Christian makes no apology for seeing the Bible as absolute truth. As followers of Jesus, we are done with relativism. Our lives are submitted to the authority of God's Word in all areas of life. This means walking by faith and in unquestioning obedience. Remember, the Christian is now out of the dark into the light of intimacy with God, free from slavery to sin in Satan's kingdom. It is now a matter of having the authority to live as a child of God (see John 1:12). This is not legalistic religiosity but real living as effective members of society, as the kind of people we really want to be, people with purpose and hope. The Christian's distinctive in life is the conscious enjoyment of God's presence and, as a result, growing to be more like Jesus. If this is not working in the constant challenges and demands of everyday living, then it is worthless. Consider some examples:

Family

There is no greater test than everyday family living. The pressures of life can bring stress to relationships in the home. Husbands and wives don't always agree how certain things ought to be handled. Trying to guide teenagers in the growing up process can create tremendous difficulties for a family. When friends call, what vibes do they feel in your home? Do they sense tension, stress, and the feeling that things are a bit out of control? Or do they sense that your family is realistic about the problems, honest about the struggles, yet peaceful through it all. If a motorist fails to pay attention to the oil level in his car, the engine eventually seizes and the vehicle grinds to a halt. On the other hand, the motorist who is conscientious about maintaining the oil level will have a car with exactly the same parts to his engine as the one which ground to a halt. The difference is the oil. All families, Christian or otherwise, are living in the same world. They all face the same challenges and frustrations. The thing that is the Christian family's distinctive is the oil of the Holy Spirit bringing harmony so the family functions smoothly. As with any vehicle, there has to be regular servicing. The family has to practise the presence of God. There is nothing more helpful to the smooth running of the family than a husband and wife who read God's Word and pray together as well as with their children.

God's Word gives clear guidelines how the family ought to function. Ephesians 5:22-33 is a key passage. One of the things which, I believe, saddens God so much is when Christian husbands do not take their role of headship seriously. I have lost count of the number of times Christian women have complained to me that their husbands will not read God's Word and pray with them. Such a situation is tragic. There is nothing that will help couples in their communication with each other like reading Scripture and praying together. This practise also results in the children feeling more secure and seeing a healthy role model for their future. The Bible nowhere even suggests that a wife is inferior to her husband when it speaks about the husband being "the head of the wife." Scripture is simply defining the God-given roles for each member of the partnership. A Christian marriage, one man and one woman to the exclusion of all others, is the creator's design (Gen. 2:24). This unique relationship was recognized by Jesus, the Son of God (Mark 10:5-9). To demonstrate that the marriage of husband and wife is the only way to go, the Holy Spirit is also involved. The Holy Spirit living inside the husband and wife is the One who unites them in a relationship, which speaks so powerfully of the relationship between Christ and His church (Eph. 5:29-30). It is the Holy Spirit living in each Christian that makes them members of Christ's body. It is an awesome concept that a marriage has each member of the Trinity involved in it. The wonderful thing about a husband and wife relationship is that each is the perfect complement of the other. Each has a distinctive role that only they can fulfill. In the various challenges of life and family, each brings a unique contribution. The one complements the other.

I grew up in a paternalistic background. The result was that in my marriage it took some time to really learn to listen to my wife. Today I'm so grateful she can bring so much to the decision-making process because of her perspective as a woman. We men need to humble ourselves and learn to take our God-given role seriously. It was Dr. James Dobson who said to husbands, "The greatest thing you can do for your children is to love their mother." Nothing brings closeness to a husband and wife relationship like reading God's Word and praying together. As you pray about the problems and challenges together, you will be able to discuss them more constructively because your discussions will be in the light of God's Word and in mutual submission to it. When this is happening, your children will pick up on it very quickly. They will sense the closeness. They will automatically feel more secure. People who visit your home will sense it too.

If you are a wife whose husband will not pray with you, gently take the lead. Let him know you are praying for him and ask if you can pray with him. If you have children, by all means, read God's Word and pray with them. I'm so grateful I had a mother who did that for my sister and me.

If you are a husband who is reticent about praying with your wife, begin simply. Write your prayer out, covering the things you feel you should bring to God. You will gain in confidence and your wife will be blessed more than you realize.

None of this will happen, of course, if you are not a couple who passionately wants to build your family on the foundation of God's Word. There is no such thing as a perfect marriage but it has been well said that any marriage can fail and any marriage can work. Love is a verb, not a noun. What an advantage it is to have a marriage built on the foundation of God's Word and permeated with the oil of the Holy Spirit.

Church Life

The fact that the Bible talks about becoming a Christian in terms of new birth demonstrates the emphasis God places on family and body life. It is clear from the New Testament that all God intends to do in the world until the return of Christ will be done through His body, His family, His church. We in the West must never spend too much time looking at depressing statistics about the seeming decline of the church. The promise of Jesus still stands and will always stand. When referring to Peter's confession, *"You are the Christ, the Son of the living God"* (Matt. 16:16-19), Jesus made a very clear statement: *"Upon this rock I will build My church and the gates of Hades will not overpower it."* Paul, speaking about God's people collectively, refers to them as a holy temple in the Lord which has been built on the foundation of the apostles and prophets, Jesus Christ Himself being the cornerstone (Eph. 2:19-22). God's building program will continue and nothing will stop it. We need to keep our vision on the universal church and not be totally preoccupied with the local church. The church is growing rapidly in places like Asia, Africa, China, and India.

Travelling on a train in England one day, I struck up a conversation with a chap who was a visitor to England from a totally different culture. I discovered he was a committed Jesus-follower and we had the most wonderful conversation together. By the time the trip was over we felt we had known each other all our lives; we really felt we were brothers in Christ. One of the many blessings in being a Christian is that you are part of Christ's body, the church universal. I remember preaching in the International Church in Tashkent, Uzbekistan. It was a thrilling experience because there were believers there who, in their daily lives, represented their home nations yet there was such a sense of all belonging to the same family of God. I happened to preach that day from John 15, which speaks of the vine and the branches. It is a Scripture that so clearly illustrates that, as believers, we are literally part of Christ, joined to Him eternally and that, as branches on the vine, it is His life that flows through each of us.

That vision of the universal church gives us a far richer appreciation of the local church. For a local church to be healthy it must be constantly aware of the universal church and have a big vision for world missions. The emphasis in the New Testament on how the local church ought to function demonstrates that God intends to do His work in the world through the local church. What we call para-church organizations should always have as part of their vision the building of the local church. It is essential that every believer be part of and involved in a church. Your church is that part of Christ's body, designed by God for His people to be able to worship with fellow believers, to be taught the Word of God and to be equipped to be effective witnesses in the world where they live and work. Through involvement at the local level, the child of God learns to discover how the Holy Spirit has gifted them, how to develop those gifts, and how best to use them to build up other members of that church.

Part of that process is seeing how they and their church family fit into the bigger picture of world missions. Your part in world missions will initially be through prayer, giving of your financial resources, and being made aware of what is going on in missions throughout the world. All the time, you will be proving yourself through contributing to the life, growth, and general well-being of your church. It will become easy for your church leadership to, happily, be part of the process, if and when you feel the call of God to missionary service. We learn from Acts 13:1-4 the importance of the local church being involved in the call of the missionary. A young missionary, planning to serve God in India, was reminded that he was not going to India to become a missionary but because he already was one. In other words, God had already been able to use him to introduce people to Jesus through his church. Others had recognized it and gave him their wholehearted support, an essential thing for any missionary.

All this is part of following God's instructions in His inspired Word, His guidebook for all matters of faith and conduct.

The World of Work

Having left Satan's kingdom in becoming part of God's kingdom means adopting a Christian worldview. It was Harry Blamires who coined the phrase popularized by Dr. John Stott, "Think Christianly." Developing a Christian worldview is impossible apart from growth in intimacy with God through the constant reading and study of His Word. The Word of God will shape our thinking. Through it we become aware of the biblical principles which must be applied to everyday living. In John 17 Jesus is praying for His disciples as they continue to live in the world. He prays that they may have His joy made full in themselves (v. 13) This is the product of intimacy with God. There is absolutely nothing to compare with the deep-seated joy that comes with such intimacy. Jesus says in the verses following that just as He is not of the world, neither are His followers. He makes it clear He is not asking that they be taken out of the world; rather, He is sending them into the world to live lives that make a difference. Such lives are sanctified. That means they are given over to God for Him to use as He determines. Such people will be effective. They will, sometimes without knowing it, positively influence people around them to seek to know Jesus too. All of us have a deep longing to live effectively. There are many people, and maybe you are one of them, who are successful in terms of material prosperity but have a feeling of not being satisfied. It is significant to see what Jesus says is the secret of this effectiveness. *"Sanctify them in the truth; Your Word is truth"* (v. 17). The Word of God is at the heart of a lifestyle that has both quality and effectiveness. The Christian who is not making God's Word the road map for life will have to settle for second best.

The Christian is Jesus' personal representative to make a difference for God's glory in the world of everyday work. To live confidently in this role, you must be totally familiar with the principles and guidelines in the roadmap. It is clear from Scripture that God's purpose for each of His children is to make them like Jesus. God is so committed to that He will turn everything that happens to us toward that end. Enjoying an intimate relationship with God does not mean trying to avoid or be taken out of challenging circumstances but rather, becoming more intimate with Him in them. That way, God will cause everything that happens to be for our good so the Christ likeness will grow (see Rom. 8:28-29). Being in the world means we will face the same challenges as the people around us who know nothing of God's love. Such people have no idea that it is possible to be intimate with the Creator of the universe. Some don't even believe He exists. It is seeing how the Christian handles life's challenges that makes the difference. First John teaches that it is God's love being reproduced in His people that enables others to see the real evidence for God (1 Jn. 4:12).

In the world of work and business, we are intended to function with godly integrity. God has put His name upon us. We are meant to be the kind of people who commend Jesus to those around us. One of the greatest discoveries I made in life is that the Lord Jesus is literally living His life in me every day (see Galatians 2:20). He does not give me things like life, joy, love and peace. He is all those things in me. Those things are the evidence of His life in the Christian. This is so freeing. Think: your whole personality permeated with the presence, the life, of the living Son of God. You want to be careful about embarking on partnerships, either in business or in marriage, with people who do not know Jesus. Your worldview is so different from theirs (2 Cor. 6:14-18). Your decision-making process will come under the guidance of biblical principles. You will prayerfully seek God's direction in the light of His Word (Ps. 32:8-9). You will sometimes seek counsel from mature Christian friends who know you well (1 Thess. 5:12). You will treat those you are responsible for, those under your authority, with respect and consideration (Col. 4:1). You will want to work for your boss in an attitude of doing your work for the glory of God first (Eph. 6:5-8). You will know the excitement of living life on the edge, risking everything on God. This is not careless or senseless risk-taking. Most older people, as they look back on their lives, wish they had, among other things, risked more. It was Dr. Tony Campolo who said, "If you never take risks you will simply arrive at your grave safely." The key words which sum up a life of intimacy with God are trust and obey. There is plenty of purpose and excitement there. Building on those principles, you will walk in peace and not in panic (Col. 3:15-16).

Finances

This is an area which is one of the greatest tests of whether we are willing to allow Christ to reign in our lives as Lord. If He is Lord, He will be Lord over our finances as well as every other area of our lives. The Bible has a lot to say about how we handle our finances. In 1 Corinthians 6:12-20, Paul talks about the Christian's body as the temple where the Holy Spirit lives. He makes the amazing statement that this means our bodies are members of Christ and that being joined to the Lord means being one spirit with Him. In talking about God being glorified in our bodies he tells us the bottom line: *"Do you not know that your body is the temple of the Holy Spirit who is in you, whom you have from God, and that you are not your own? For you have been bought with a price: therefore glorify God in your body"* (1 Cor. 6:19-20). Not being our own involves allowing Jesus to be Lord over our bank account. This brings such peace and contentment because we will be out of debt and will experience the thrill of seeing how the Lord supplies all our needs. There is something very special about being able to look back on a year with holy surprise when we realise how God has been so faithful. All we have needed was supplied; we have no debt and we have given more money than ever to the work of the Lord.

Realizing we are not our own because our lives are under the direction of the Lord Jesus solves the problem of how much money we give to the Lord's work throughout the world. It is no longer a question of how much but rather, "Everything is Yours Lord. I gladly give as much as You ask me to give. After all, You gave everything to redeem me, to make me part of Your eternal kingdom (2 Cor. 8:9). I know You have promised to supply everything I need as I faithfully give. I will not be treating You like a spiritual stock exchange, investing with the return in mind. You want to abundantly supply what I need so that I can be more abundant in my giving" (Prov. 3:9-10; Phil. 4:10-20; 2 Cor. 9:1-15). The Macedonian Christians were poor and persecuted, yet their giving was generous and with joy. What was their secret? Quite simply, they first gave themselves to the Lord (2 Cor. 8:5) I remember being taken by surprise when preaching in a Pentecostal church in Trinidad some years ago. When the pastor announced it was time to take the offering, the whole congregation burst into loud applause! Although poor people, they had caught the joy of giving to the Lord.

Giving a tenth can be a good place to start. A pastor-friend calculated that if every member of his congregation were on welfare and still gave only a tenth, there would never be any shortage of money for the work of the Lord in his community and beyond.

Leisure Time

God puts great emphasis on a day of rest, the Sabbath. Jesus invited His disciples to take time to rest. The apostles in the book of Acts saw the value of this. Paul's strategy for ministry under the direction of the Holy Spirit took him on various missionary journeys; however, there was always time for rest and renewal (Acts 14:24-28). Jesus is the Good Shepherd. The Bible picture of Him leading His sheep is one of the sheep being led through green pastures and beside quiet waters so the shepherd can restore the soul (Ps. 23). What a delightful picture! There will be no rewards in heaven if you burn out for Jesus. I learned this the hard way. Burn out in the service of Jesus is the antithesis of the will of the Lord for His servants. He wants us not only to have planned periods of rest and renewal but He also wants us to be at rest while serving Him (Matt. 11:29-30).

How the Christian spends his or her leisure time should be governed by the benefit to be derived. Leisure does not necessarily mean doing nothing; it can mean doing something different. Philippians 4:8 gives some guidelines: *"whatever is true, whatever is honorable, whatever is right, whatever is pure, whatever is lovely, whatever is of good repute, if there is any excellence and if anything worthy of praise, dwell on these things."* There is plenty of scope there for wholesome leisure activity. Things outside such guidelines produce neither rest nor restoration.

Conclusion

Life is so demanding. There are constant demands on our time and energy. When we stand before the Lord, telling Him we did not have time for His Word will carry no weight. We can find time for the things we want to do. Many of us, because we are not spending adequate time in God's Word, have little idea of how rich our lives could be in all the areas dealt with in this chapter. The challenge is to bring each area under the scrutiny of God's Word. This means we must say no to some things so we can say yes to God in others.

Something to Ponder

Life may be demanding but I can't afford not to have time for God's Word. It is only in intimacy with God that I can learn how much He wants to bless me in all areas of life and service.

EIGHT

I Have So Much on My Mind

Winning the battle for our minds is crucial if we are going to grow in intimacy with God. The Bible speaks of *"taking every thought captive to the obedience of Christ"* (2 Cor. 10:5). The first thing to happen when we surrender everything to Christ as Lord is that we are transformed by the renewing of [our] mind (Rom. 12:2). We think differently about everything. Intimacy with God is impossible without this. Producing such a mind is the Holy Spirit's work. Paul points out some things about the Christian mind in 1 Corinthians 2. The bottom line is that the Christian's faith does *"not rest on the wisdom of men, but on the power of God"* (1 Cor. 2:5). He tells us the person who does not have the Holy Spirit cannot understand the things of the Spirit of God. There is absolutely no way to understand what is available to the true Jesus-follower other than through the Holy Spirit. But the amazing thing is that when God's Holy Spirit is in us, we have the mind of Christ (1 Cor. 2:16). Stop and allow the significance of that statement to sink in. It's amazing. The possibilities it opens up in terms of God's truth being revealed to us are boundless.

Meditation

Using the intellect is very important in thinking Christianly. We must use our minds for God's glory. Obviously, some are more intellectually inclined than others but the one thing that is available to every Christian is the ability to meditate on God's Word. This kind of meditation is a lost art. We are not talking about meditation as a mystical exercise, we are talking about the Christian's mind being filled with God's thoughts from God's Word. Thus, God can reveal His great truths which result in true intimacy with Himself, which results in the ongoing transformation of the life. The Chambers' 20th Century Dictionary defines to meditate as "to consider thoughtfully, to consider deeply, reflect upon: to revolve in the mind." It is not rocket science to work out that such an exercise involves time and effort. The devil wins a great victory when you allow your mind to be undisciplined and filled with other stuff, leaving no time to meditate on God's Word. Who you are when alone is who you truly are. What fills your mind in those moments when you are alone? Do your thoughts turn almost automatically to what you have been reading in God's Word? You think your greatest thoughts when meditating on God's breathed-out Word. This is your allowing the Holy Spirit to be your teacher. As Jesus said, *"He will lead you into all truth"* (John 16:13).

The Quietness Factor

For whatever reason, people today seem to find it almost impossible to live with quietness. Students study in noisy coffee shops and people walk with music playing in their ears. We have to endure music, even if it is not to our liking, when having a meal in a restaurant. We live in a very noisy world. In the Chapel of St. Faith in Westminster Abbey there is complete silence. If you have ever had a harrowing day in London, England, battling with crowds and the roar of the London traffic, a few minutes in this little chapel gives a whole new meaning to the idea of quietness. It is a healing and restorative haven. Psalm 107 speaks several times about the loving kindness of the Lord and the wonders He has performed on His people's behalf. It paints the picture of a storm at sea and then it says, *"He caused the storm to be still, so that the waves of the sea were hushed. Then they were glad because they were quiet, so He guided them to their desired haven"* (Ps. 107:29-30). In Isaiah 30 God says, *"In repentance and rest you will be saved, in quietness and trust is your strength."* The Good Shepherd leads His sheep in green pastures and beside quiet waters (Ps. 23).

Quietness of mind and heart, peace in the innermost being, is inevitable in a relationship with God.

To be serious about meditation, we must learn to be quiet. God wants to speak into our lives. Following his conflict with the prophets of Baal, Elijah did not hear God in the wind, the fire, or the earthquake but in the *"gentle whisper"* (1 Kgs. 19:12 NIV). To hear the quiet voice of the Holy Spirit, we must select a place where we can be undisturbed and alone with God on a daily basis. If you are part of a large and busy family or if, like me, you travel a lot, you will have to be creative in finding a quiet place. You will soon realize you are in a battle. You will have to battle with things like laziness, excuses, demanding people, and things which are urgent but not important. This battle has to be won. Losing this battle is the reason for so much defeat and weakness in the Christian church. Good habits, like regularly being alone with God, have to be worked at. But the results soon become noticeable to you and to those around you. You cannot be intimate with God and hide the fact.

The Intimacy Factor

It is impossible to develop intimacy with God without great changes becoming apparent. Here are some examples of things to look for, things that were impossible before the intimacy factor:

- It will seem you have more time for the other stuff of life.
- Your appetite for God's Word will grow.
- You will realize why the Bible says God's peace "surpasses all comprehension" because you will be unusually peaceful.
- *"The joy of the Lord is your strength"* (Neh. 8:10). This will surprise you.
- You will know when God has spoken into your life.
- You will see people around you through different eyes and you will want to share your walk with God with them in a sensitive way.

- You will experience greater victory over personal sin.
- You will be far more sensitive to the things that grieve the Holy Spirit.
- You will have a far greater sense of hope.
- The focus of your life will no longer be you, but Christ; who is your life (see Col. 3:1-4).

One of the Creator's great gifts is the gift of memory. The memory can be trained and that process can be a significant aid in meditating on God's Word and consequently, developing the intimacy factor. I have been especially helped over the years in using the Navigators' system of Scripture memorization (www.navigators.ca or www.navigators.org). A Bible verse is printed on one side of a small card, with the scripture reference on the other. You can carry your cards with you. At all kinds of odd moments, like standing in a line, sitting on a bus, train, or plane, or out walking, you can take out the cards and work through them. Read the words, try to remember the reference, then reverse the procedure. Not only will you be storing up scripture in your mind, you will discover this to be a helpful way to meditate on God's Word. Times when your mind would formerly have been filled with unhelpful thoughts will now be times of intimacy with God.

Being a Jesus-follower means that developing your relationship with Him is the number one priority of life. It is a question of living each day in an attitude of willing obedience. To use the biblical expression, it is a question of devotion to the Lord (1 Cor. 7:25). You will very quickly realize that meditation on scripture is a two-way street. As you, remembering the dictionary definition of meditation, consider God's Word thoughtfully and deeply, reflecting upon it and revolving it in your mind, you will be hearing from God and realizing the relevance of God's Word to where you are in life's journey. You will soon find your prayer life beginning to take on another dimension as you take the fruit of your meditation and pray it back to the Lord. Out of that, you will find the Holy Spirit directing your thoughts in prayer. You will sense your praying becoming much more powerful and passionate. This is part of what the Bible means when it speaks of praying in the Spirit (Eph. 6:18). There is nothing more exciting than intimacy with the living God. That is why the devil's greatest concentration of activity in any Christian's life is in the area of trying to destroy intimacy with God. The Christian who is intimate with the Lord is powerful and effective. When Moses had spent a prolonged time in the presence of God, he was unaware that his face was shining. The glory of God will be upon the Christian's life when the intimacy factor is real.

The Healing Factor

Meditation on God's Word is important because the process allows the Holy Spirit to invade the deepest recesses of life. The disciple is quiet in the Lord's presence, thinking deeply and praying over what is being read. Nothing is hidden, no area is kept closed. The Holy Spirit is able to say the things that need to be said and reveal the things that need to be revealed. Those are truly sacred moments when transactions are taking place between God and the humble, submissive soul. There may be deeply entrenched hurts, anger, or bitterness. There may be some area of constant defeat. Deep healing can take place in those holy moments.

Few of us realize the enormous power inherent in the God-breathed words of Holy Scripture. When God speaks, we can expect things to happen. The universe was created by the word of the Lord (Gen. 1). He sent His Word and healed His troubled people (Ps. 107:20). Jesus spoke and people were healed; some were raised from the dead (Mark 2:1-13; John 11:1-46). God still speaks and you and I have what He is saying in our hands and we have Him living inside us. This is of stupendous significance (that is no exaggeration). If you are a disciple of Jesus, this is true of you at this moment:

"For thus says the high and exalted One who lives forever, whose name is Holy, 'I dwell on a high and holy place, and also with the contrite and lowly of spirit in order to revive the spirit of the lowly and to revive the heart of the contrite'" (Isa. 57:15).

God is waiting to do His healing work through His Word as we allow Him to speak into the hidden areas of our being.

The Eternity Factor

One of my sons asked what I thought things would be like if Christians really believed all they say they believe. I have thought a great deal about his question and have come to the conclusion there are many things to which we give only mental assent. This is a serious situation because it means today's church, especially in Western cultures, is like the church in Laodicea—neither cold nor hot. God had some stern words for such a church. He said He would spit them out of His mouth (Rev. 3:16). Allow me to put you to the test as you read. What is your reaction to the following statement: *"The form of this world is passing away"* (1 Cor. 7:31). The world as we know it is on its way out; that is what he is saying. The Laodicean mindset in today's church will never change until we stop saying we believe in eternity while still hanging on to our worldly stuff as though it was forever. We must recover the eternity factor. All God did for the world through Christ was, primarily, to make it possible for us to change our eternal destiny. Knowing Jesus as personal Saviour means to be made alive to God, to share His eternal life. It means the whole of life changes direction and purpose. Instead of living for the stuff of this present world, which is on its way out, life's focus becomes walking with God. Priorities change. Things are held lightly. People are seen potentially as becoming radically different if only they would come to faith in Christ. We must understand that our totally unique Bible, this God-breathed Word, was by nature, spoken out of eternity. The passion in God's heart is there. That the people He created be reconciled to Him by being brought from eternal death to eternal life is the heart of its message. To say we know God through Jesus, while still living as though the world's temporary things were the most important, is a contradiction in terms. Be done with mental assent alone, live as men and women who truly believe God. The focus of our lives must be on being holy and not just happy. The motivation behind everything we do must be a confident and expectant longing for the return of Christ as we live effective and fruitful lives in the power of the Holy Spirit.

Something to Ponder

The eternity factor is important. All disciples of Jesus will be held accountable (see Rom. 14:10-12; 1 Cor. 3:10-23) and be rewarded for the quality of their service in Jesus' name. Are you looking forward to that or do you feel the need of the healing factor?

NINE

A Healthy Appetite and Regular Exercise

Sometimes a meal of just a couple of appetizers can be very enjoyable, but it would be unwise to eat like that constantly. The main course is where the real nourishment is. The intimacy factor in our relationship with God is, as we have seen, something to be developed, something to grow into. But make no mistake, the aim is to develop a day-by-day, hour-by-hour, moment-by-moment intimacy where the habit of interacting with God becomes as natural as breathing. If this sounds daunting, enjoy some appetizers for a time. You must get beyond intimacy with God being seen as a religious thing. If that is how you view it, your time with God will not be time with God at all, but merely another of your many chores. The last thing you need is more chores.

Begin with Five Minutes

Bearing in mind all we have said about finding a quiet place to be alone with God, it is helpful to begin in a small way. This will help get over the whole idea being so daunting that we never get to it. Five minutes is a long time if it is used profitably. The bottom line is, are you motivated? The chances are that if you are reading this book you are. Should it be, however, that becoming motivated is your problem, honestly take the matter to God in prayer. People often say they go through times when they either cannot or they find it difficult to pray. The remedy is to tell God about it because as soon as you do, you have begun to pray. So it is with motivation. Intimacy with God is exactly that, the kind of relationship where nothing is hidden. There is total honesty and a willingness to be transparent with God. Make five minutes for God. It will be your most important investment of time ever. The five minutes will soon expand as your time with God becomes richer and more meaningful.

I remember being challenged about this while sitting in an airport lounge. There were some Muslims waiting to board the same flight. Part of their waiting time was spent by taking out their prayer mats, getting on their knees and praying toward Mecca. Travelling sometimes means being in airports at all times of the day or night. There are rich times of intimacy with God to be had by learning to be alone in a crowd so as to spend time in God's Word.

Structuring Five Minutes

Begin with a few seconds of quiet prayer, asking that the Holy Spirit open your eyes to what God wants you to see in His Word (see Ps. 119:18). Read a few verses or a paragraph in your Bible for about three minutes. Ask yourself what you feel you have learned from what you have just read. Spend the last minute thanking God for what you have received from His Word, turning it into a time of prayer. You will pray about applying what you have learned to your life. You will also be directed to pray for other situations in light of what you have learned. Remember, nothing is too insignificant to share with your heavenly Father.

There Is Help Available

One of the four gospels is a good place to begin if you don't have another reading plan. However, there are many helpful plans available, so you will truly grow through your times with God. Simply Google Daily Bread, In Touch Ministries, Scripture Union or Every Day With Jesus. The resources available from these helpful sites are hugely beneficial. You may receive further help by keeping a journal of what you learn from God's Word. Reviewing this from time to time will encourage you as you see how much you have grown.

To help with meditation on whatever scripture you may be reading, ask questions at the end of your reading time. Questions like:

What have I learned about God, Jesus, or the Holy Spirit?

What have I learned about myself?

Is there anything I feel God is telling me to do or not to do?

Is the Holy Spirit prompting me to pray about an issue?

Is there someone I know with whom I ought to share what God has said to me today? If you can't think of someone, ask the Lord to direct you to the right person.

Things to Watch Out For

Your daily time with God is, without a doubt, the most important and exciting thing in your schedule. After all, you are hearing from Almighty God about growing in your relationship with Him. This is a spiritual exercise; if you are at all serious about growing in your relationship with God, you will have realized already you are in a battle. The devil will do whatever it takes to stop your daily time with the Lord. The battle of the urgent against the important will become more intense. Remember, nothing is more important than your walk with God. Get that right and you will move toward being the kind of person you really want to be. You will become successful as God measures success. Most of us know there are people who are truly successful as far as the world measures success. They are wealthy and seem to have everything the heart could desire. Yet, in the really important areas of life they are walking disasters. Godly success includes having a deep-seated sense of wholeness, purpose, and hope. It means a family life where, together with all the challenges, there is love, mutual respect, and care for one another. It means having the resources to cope with things like health challenges and tragedy. Perhaps most importantly, it means having that precious possession, without which none of us can really live—hope. When God told Joshua to make meditating on His Word a priority, His promise was, *"Then you will make your way prosperous, and then you will have success*" (Josh. 1:8). It is only when, by the grace of God, we have been taken from the kingdom of darkness into the kingdom of God that we begin to understand the meaning of true success. It is the most logical, the most exciting thing in the world—being reconciled to our Creator will mean successful living and hope-filled dying.

This daily battle for our time and minds must be won. Realizing that Jesus, by the Holy Spirit, is living in you is a major step forward. Surrender your mind and time to Him; draw upon His life within you. This is the key to victory over the things that bring us into defeat and about which we must be constantly mindful. Be totally honest with yourself about your greatest personal weakness and constantly look out for things like:

Laziness—do you sleep more than you need to?

Lack of discipline—are you constantly defeated by the urgent?

Overindulgence—do you watch too much TV?

Wrong use of time—are there things you need to cut out?

In our spiritual life as well as in any other area of life, the old adage applies, "If I aim at nothing, I'll hit it every time."

TEN

Moving On to Peak Condition

It's amazing the amount of wooly thinking there is regarding the idea of walking by faith. Some give the impression that a person who talks about living by faith is a lesser mortal who hasn't quite got it all together. I go back to the picture of the air traveller who, each time he or she boards a plane, makes an informed decision to trust the engineers and pilots. The Christian, in walking by faith, does not abandon his or her mind in the process. The Christian, as we have seen, has very good reasons for walking by faith. For example, the Bible tells us that the Christian is saved by grace through faith (Eph. 2:8) and that we walk by faith and not by sight (2 Cor. 5:7). God has taken the initiative and has done all that needs to be done. He has demonstrated the validity of it all by raising Jesus from the dead. True faith is informed faith. It rejoices in the plentiful evidence, justifying it, and then trusts God, no matter what. The mind is important. Thank God for those whose intellect has been brought to bear upon the study of God's Word and yet have balanced that with a child-like faith that is prepared to take God at His Word and, as a result, prove Him in experience. Such people are gifts of God to the church.

It is so important to see that faith has a crucial part to play in cultivating a meaningful walk with God. If no time is spent in reading and studying God's Word, there will be little faith; what faith there is will be extremely weak. *"Faith comes from hearing and hearing from the word of Christ,"* Romans 10:17 tells us. This is why it is such an enormous responsibility to stand before a congregation, claiming to be preaching or teaching God's Word.

The object of the exercise is to see faith created in the hearts of the hearers. This is how Paul viewed his ministry: *"My message and my preaching were not in persuasive words of wisdom, but in demonstration of the Spirit and of power, so that your faith would not rest on the wisdom of men, but on the power of God"* (1 Cor. 2:4-5). To experience the power of God you must learn to walk by faith. God says He has given the Holy Spirit to those who obey Him (Acts 5:32). Thank God for your intellect. Use it, stretch it, think Christianly but, whatever you do, get beyond it to faith that ventures everything on God. The plain fact of the matter is that it is impossible to please God without faith (Heb. 11:6). The essence of the Christian life is what God does by the Holy Spirit in and then through the individual, not what the individual does for God. Being a Christian means Jesus is living inside you; progress is impossible apart from allowing Him to do just that. The bottom line is your complete and absolute surrender to Him and a willingness to trust Him with a simple, child-like faith. There may well be times in your experience when all you have left is raw faith and you can only cling to God by your fingernails. Keep clinging. God will prove faithful to His promises—that is what keeps you clinging. If you are unfamiliar with the great promises of God, your faith will be correspondingly less.

Faith and Worry

When you are anxious, perhaps over a family crisis, God's promise is that as you demonstrate your trust in Him by bringing the matter to Him in prayer, He will give you a peace that will surprise you (Phil. 4:6-7). By prayer, God means rolling the burden onto Him with a trusting heart. That is walking by faith. That means being willing to totally commit your family member to God, trusting Him to do what needs to be done, not your trying to do God's work for Him.

Faith and Temptation

In temptation, you may be tempted to do something dishonest or immoral. You may be tempted to become involved in an extramarital affair, to look at stuff on television or on the

Internet you know is wrong. You may be tempted to steal time or something else from your boss. Your daily time in God's Word will be a tremendous source of strength and encouragement (so will real fellowship with fellow believers). God has given us a specific promise for just such a challenge. In 1 Corinthians 10:13, He tells us we are not alone in being tempted, that He will be faithful to us, that He will not allow us to be tempted beyond what we can cope with and, when temptation comes, He will make a way of escape so we can endure it. God promises victory. Walking by faith in temptation means listening to God's voice rather than your's. Most of us are good at justifying sin in our lives. Walking by faith while in temptation means focusing on our risen Lord Jesus and realizing that He has already won the battle we think we have to fight every day. If our focus is on ourselves or the world, things could be pretty depressing (Heb. 2:8). But if our focus is on the risen Lord Jesus, everything changes because *"we do see Him who was made for a little while lower than the angels, namely Jesus, because of the suffering of death crowned with glory and honor, so that by the grace of God He might taste death for everyone"* (Heb. 2:9). It's like saying we won when our favourite team wins a game.

Years ago, when our two boys were much younger, I was watching a cup final game with them. Totenham Hotspur and Manchester United were the two teams. Phil was a Manchester man and Tim was a Totenham man. I was sitting between them! Totenham won that day, and, at the conclusion of the game, Tim rushed to his mom yelling, 'we won.' Even though he wasn't even in the stadium, never mind playing in the game, he was so closely identified with Totenham that, as far as he was concerned, their victory was his too.

Because our focus is on our victorious Lord, we can say we won. When your whole life is surrendered to Jesus so He is undisputed Lord of every part, then, in the moment of temptation, you surrender everything to Him, making Him Lord of the moment. As Romans 12:2 teaches, we know what it means to be *"transformed by the renewing of our mind."* The Holy Spirit changes the attitude and thought pattern the moment the situation is yielded to Him.

Faith and Anger

There are many things going on in today's world that will make you angry because they are just plain wrong. But there is another kind of anger which ought to have no place in the life of the Jesus-follower. This anger is dishonouring to the Lord Jesus and ought never be part of the Christian's daily walk. The Bible speaks about anger in Ephesians 4 in the context of what it means to walk with Jesus. It makes it clear that when we do become angry, we don't have to keep the anger in our hearts. We must not do that. We have the resources to deal with the anger; we can deal with the anger quickly without allowing it to fester in our hearts (Eph. 4:26). The bumper sticker which says, "Do not let the sun go down while you are still angry, stay up all night and fight" is not good theology! The point is: being in God's Word is where we find out how to apply the simple steps so the anger is dealt with. Ephesians 4 teaches this in the context of the truth that is in Jesus, that is in His Word. The simple steps:

> *"lay aside the old self"* (v. 22)
> *"be renewed in the spirit of your mind"* (v. 23)
> *"put on the new self"* (v. 24)

This is only possible because Jesus, by the Holy Spirit, is living inside the believer. Because of this, we can stop the devil using our anger to gain a foothold in our lives. Allowing him to gain that foothold leads to something else, anger which leads to bitterness, wrath, slander, and malice. Such anger is destructive in the life of the angry person. But more importantly, it grieves the Holy Spirit because what is produced in the life is the antithesis of everything the Holy Spirit wants to produce. The relationship with God and others is badly damaged and so is the angry person's testimony in the eyes of others. It is important to realize that as long as you hold on to anger and bitterness, you will make no progress in your walk with God, and the rich treasure contained in God's Word will remain hidden. If you are such a person, take a bold step of faith today. Change your mind and agree with God about the anger and bitterness being wrong and harmful. Repent of it, turn from it, renounce it completely, and make things right with the person you are angry with. If that person is no longer alive, share the matter with a mature Christian who knows you well and receive advice how you can lay down the burden once and for all.

It is so important to understand that things like anger, lust, covetousness and pride are huge weights around the neck of the Christian. Real growth simply will not happen until such things are dealt with. In Hebrews chapter 12, where we are taught that God will stop at nothing to have us mature as His children, we are told He disciplines us so we may share His holiness. For that to happen, Hebrews 12 tells us such weights must be put away so we can run like a totally free and unhindered athlete with our focus on Jesus alone. After all, He is the one who did all that needs to be done to make this superbly qualitative lifestyle, the life of faith, possible.

Something to Ponder

It ought to be obvious that to live life on the edge means having a faith that is vital, growing in your walk with God, and enjoying victory over sin and the things that, up till now, have pulled you down. What things, if any, in your life are weights around your neck, things that hinder your progress as a follower of Jesus? What do you plan to do about it?

ELEVEN

I'm Finding I Need Help

A primary mark of a disciple of Jesus Christ is having the whole of life governed by the principles in God's Word. That obviously means time spent in the reading and studying those precious, God-breathed words. Such study is the most exciting and rewarding investment of any Christian's time. No experience compares with those moments when, as a result of diligent study, the Holy Spirit lights up some truth in Scripture so it is woven into the fabric of your life. You can take ownership of that truth in what is undoubtedly a sanctified moment. Your study time becomes a worship time. No matter what else may be going on in life, that sanctified moment is so freeing. Though current circumstances may be extremely difficult, there is a deep-seated joy even where there is no happiness. Holiness and happiness don't always go together, but holiness and joy always do.

There is a tendency today to major on being honest about our trials and failings. While I am not suggesting we be other than totally honest, there is a far greater need to be Christ-centred, not problem-centred. The kind of study of God's Word being talked about here has the effect of making the student much less self-centred. Always talking about and airing problems is a subtle form of self-centredness. Studying God's Word will very soon produce in the disciple complete agreement with Scripture when it says, *"by the grace of God I am what I am"* (1 Cor. 15:10). The kind of student of the Bible God is looking for is the one who is *"humble and contrite of spirit* [deeply sorry for sin] *one who trembles at* [His] *word"* (Isa. 66:2). Such a person will live in the constant awareness that he or she deserves none of the blessings they have in Christ. They will always be in an attitude of worship to the God of amazing grace.

Jesus perfectly summed it up when talking to some believing Jews one day: *"If you continue in My word then you are truly disciples of Mine; and you will know the truth and the truth will make you free"* (John 8:31-32).

For this kind of study, it is important to acquire some helpful tools. There is no real substitute for building a library of study books. Over the years, they will become your friends, always available to be dipped into. Although this means financial outlay, it is an investment which will remain profitable into eternity. Many study tools can be easily accessed through the Internet, www.Biblegateway.com for example.

Your Study Bible

I can still sense the excitement when I first learned how to use my study Bible as I discovered how to follow a theme through Scripture. To do this, it is important to acquire a good-sized Bible with marginal references. A Bible with wide margins is important, as will soon become apparent.

Various words in the text of such a Bible will either be lettered or numbered. The letters or numbers can be traced to the page margin where other references are listed. Following those references through Scripture leads to a better understanding of that particular theme. When done prayerfully, with a willingness to meditate on what is being read, the Holy Spirit will begin to do exactly what Jesus said He would do—lead you into a deeper understanding of God's truth. During this process, what is learned can be neatly noted in the wide margin. It is helpful to make detailed notes of what is learned in a notebook.

Having copies of the Bible in various good translations is helpful; you can study some Bible book or part of a book by reading it in various translations. This gives a better sense of the main message of the part of Scripture being studied.

A Concordance

Next to a study Bible, this is the most important tool. A good concordance has more uses than just finding a particular verse in the Bible. It is so useful for learning the meanings of various words in context. A variety of words in the original Hebrew (Old Testament) or Greek (New Testament) may be translated by the same English word. A good concordance will reveal where the various words in the original languages are used. This kind of word study is very rewarding. The following concordances are recommended:

Young's Analytical Concordance of the Holy Bible, based on the King James Version

Strong's Exhaustive Concordance of the Bible, with key-word comparisons between the KJV and five other contemporary translations

NIV Complete Concordance, for students using the New International Version of the Bible

For Word Studies

As mentioned, word studies can be hugely rewarding. Understanding what the original writers meant by using a particular word will lead to a much deeper understanding of Scripture. Various tools are available for this kind of study; I mention two:

The Expository Dictionary of New Testament Words by W. E. Vine

The Theological Dictionary of the New Testament, edited by Kittel and Friedrich. Some knowledge of New Testament Greek is essential to benefit from this one.

Bible Dictionaries

A good Bible dictionary is invaluable when it comes to studying specific Bible topics. I recommend the Illustrated Bible Dictionary, published by InterVarsity Press.

Bible Atlas

There are many on the market. To purchase a better quality one is an excellent investment.

Commentaries

Good commentaries on the various books of the Bible by reputable scholars are a wise investment. The Tyndale series published by IVP is especially recommended. Using these in the study of God's Word is time well spent. There are also one-volume commentaries of the entire Bible on the market.

The Original Languages

The more serious Bible student will want to become as proficient as possible in the original languages of the Bible, Hebrew and Greek. To study these so you can handle some of the study tools more efficiently is so worthwhile.

Theology

Another fruitful and important field of Bible study is in the foundational doctrines of the faith—doctrines like God, Scripture, man, sin, the person of Christ, the work of Christ, the Holy Spirit, the church and the second advent of Christ. An excellent aid to such study is The New Dictionary of Theology, published by IVP.

The correct use of study tools such as these adds so much to experiencing the richness of God's Word. For it to be a truly nourishing study, the mind must first be satisfied and then the heart. It is important to be intellectually honest, but the primary object of the exercise remains intimacy with God through Christ. His truth has to get to the heart via the mind.

A few years ago a lady phoned to tell me that, at last she understood what I had been trying to tell her for some time. She saw, as never before, that Christ was literally living in her. "Its wonderful", she said. "It has moved from my head down into my heart."

If you are wondering where to start, I suggest beginning

with John's gospel. There you will discover who Jesus is. From there, move to Philippians, the epistle of joy. From knowing who He is, you will move to the joy of Christ being your very life. As you study Philippians, you will see that:

Living within you, Christ is at the centre of everything (1:21).

This means your attitude to everything changes (2:5).

Then your ambitions in life change (3:10).

And, no matter what life may throw at you, He is your strength (4:13).

A Challenge

Visit a Christian bookstore and browse through some of the books suggested in this chapter. Prayerfully consider budgeting for Bible study. No sacrifice can be too great or more worthwhile.

TWELVE

Your World Needs to Know about This

If you want to add to the richness, the joy, and the immense satisfaction of studying the God-breathed Scriptures you must see the exercise in the light of equipping yourself so the Lord can work through you to touch others. What you are going to learn is far too good to keep to yourself. The process of developing intimacy with God means He works in you, constantly changing you from the inside out. He works in you so He can work through you. Holy people are whole people, those whose lives speak well of Jesus. They are people your world needs to know. Don't be hung up on who you think you ought to be; just be who you are, filled with Jesus, and watch Him do the rest. Renounce the proud attitude of, "I'm not good enough." We know that anyway; none of us is. But with Christ living in us, we are dynamite. God will always use a surrendered life.

One of the reasons studying the Bible has become a chore for you as a professing Christian: you have lost sight of the fact that all your reading and study of God's Word has to be done in the context of becoming more effective as salt and light in the world. When the Bible is life-changing for you, you will make a difference in your world. This is why so many followers of Jesus can stand up under severe persecution and do it with joy and peace filling their hearts. This is what keeps the daily time with God and His Word so meaningful and relevant for everyday living. If you are not enjoying that daily time with God, you will only see making a difference like everyone else, in terms of doing good. There is absolutely nothing wrong with doing good, but for you, doing good has the added dimension of being a means to introducing someone to the Lord Jesus. This can be scary, not because you don't want to introduce people to Jesus but because you don't feel equipped to face the challenge. There is nothing complicated about this. It is simply a matter of whatever is filling you on the inside has to come out in actions, words, or sometimes both. If your life is filled with Jesus, He will be seen in how you live and in what you say. Making a difference becomes inevitable.

Telling Your Story

Everyone has a story to tell. Each person's experience of life and of God is their own. This is one of the reasons the Bible speaks in terms of God causing all things to work together for good to those who love God (Rom. 8:28). His great purpose for each of His children is that they be like Jesus (Rom. 8:29). Going through the challenging times of life with God and the strengthening of His Word is so much better than not. Such experience of God simply cannot be hidden. Why do you think the Bible challenges the Christian to be thankful in everything (1 Thess. 5:18)? Because whatever the experiences of life, God uses them to make us more Christ-like. This simply cannot be hidden. Such people have a story to tell. Telling your story may simply mean sharing something God gave you from His Word, if your circumstances and the other person's are similar. It is amazing the difference telling your story makes in that context, especially when you add that you will be praying for your friend with real empathy.

God and His Word proved to be so real during all the years of my wife's dreadful depression, which almost destroyed us and our marriage. It has led to our being able to bless all kinds of people through telling our story.

Telling your story could also be relating the relevance of your faith in Christ to someone who is asking questions, having seen the quality of your life over time. A very high percentage of people who turn to Christ do so primarily because of what they have seen of Jesus in a Christian. God's Word tells us to be ready to give an answer to people who ask the reason for the difference in our lives (1 Pet. 3:15). That difference is seen because we are people of hope. Again, if I am not spending daily time in God's Word, I will never be ready because there will be very little evidence of anything different about my life. Also, I won't even want anyone to ask me such questions, never mind give them any sort of answer. It is that closeness to the Lord Jesus that brings about the ongoing change in the life. It's what the Bible calls growing in grace (2 Pet. 3:18). Such growing simply cannot be hidden because what is in the heart comes out in the life. A person close to Jesus has His glory about them; they look different. Although far from perfect, they are more peaceful, more joyful, less moody, more compassionate. In other words, more like Jesus!

When I left school to start my banking career, I was advised by a mature Christian to nail my colors to the mast at the earliest opportunity. I so longed to be worthy of my Saviour at work and I remember praying earnestly that the Lord would help me to speak well of Him. I was amazed at how quickly and effectively God answered that prayer. Once the people in the office knew I was a committed Christian, things became easier and also more difficult. Easier because I had crossed a bridge, but more difficult because there was the daily challenge to be consistent. Some days, I left the office feeling so ashamed at how I had let the Lord down by a bad attitude or by something I had said. Other days, I was just thrilled at how the Lord had been so faithful in enabling me not to be ashamed of Him. God gave me all kinds of opportunities to talk to people about what it meant to be a Christian, people in my office or those I met on the bus. It was on the bus I did most of my Scripture memorizing. Looking back on those days when I was in my late teens and early twenties, I think I overdid things with some people. There was too much preaching and not enough telling my story.

Most Christians have had the experience of thinking of their best answers after the event. Those are learning experiences. It means you have time to think things through and then give a better answer the next time. Simply telling your story relates your Christian experience to real life. This is important for the person who is interested in what it means to be a follower of Jesus. In telling your story there are a few important things to keep in mind if you really want to help the person:

Humility—We Christians are far from perfect and we deserve none of the good things God has brought into our lives since we came to faith in Christ. It is all by the grace of God (1 Cor. 15:10). Giving the impression of superiority and talking down to someone does nothing to help them come to faith in Christ.

Love—Someone once said that if I care, I will communicate. Genuine love and concern for people and where they are going to be in eternity will do more than anything to ensure we communicate effectively. If you saw someone in great danger and had but a few seconds to warn them, you would use the simplest language possible and it would be obvious that you cared.

Honesty—We must earn the right to tell someone our story. That is partly what the apostle Peter had in mind when he spoke about giving an answer to anyone who asks the reason for the hope within the believer in Jesus. If I claim to be a follower of Jesus, people have the right to watch my life for evidence of that claim. Going back to Peter again, the context where he speaks about people asking the reason for our hope is that of having set apart Christ as Lord. When you make Jesus Lord in your life, you soon realize you are in a battle. The devil will do all he can to destroy your testimony in the eyes of others. It is so important to understand the need to use what God has provided if you are going to remain strong:

> *"The belt of truth, the breastplate of righteousness, the preparation of the gospel of peace, the shield of faith, the helmet of salvation, and the sword of the Spirit"* (Eph. 6:10-17).

Any Christian who gives the impression that faith in Jesus means all their problems are solved and life is now one big celebration is lying. There are many professing Christians who have more problems and defeats than they need because they are focused more on themselves or on their problems rather than on Jesus. There is a tendency to think there is virtue in always airing problems. There is not. People know life is full of problems and they know what the problems are. It simply helps a lot when the Christian sharing their story identifies with the problems and is honest about the struggles in certain areas. It is especially helpful if we can identify with our friend's problem because we have been there and done that and are not always winning the battle. However, sharing your story is not a psychology lesson; the object of the exercise is to focus that person on the Lord Jesus. By all means, be honest about the problems and the struggles, but tell how Christ, living inside you, is making such a difference and that you are becoming stronger as you grow in your relationship with Him. God's Word is so honest. If you spend time in it, you will be too.

Clarity—Years ago I had the wonderful privilege of introducing a Chinese doctor to Jesus. He later introduced his wife to Jesus by telling her what I had told him. Obviously, this man was highly intelligent, in a different league from me; the last thing I wanted to do was insult his intelligence. The gospel is simple but not simplistic. The gospel never insults the intelligence. The big lesson is, as Scripture says, the gospel *"is the power of God for salvation to everyone who believes"* (Rom. 1:16). The Chinese doctor knew very little English so I spoke to him through a translator. It was essential to keep things simple. It is important to understand that the Holy Spirit does not use my version of the gospel, but God's Word. It is when we try to give our version, in an attempt to help someone, that we complicate things. People need to hear God's version. After all, their need is critical. They are in great danger because where they will be for eternity is at stake. It is good to know we can give God's version, the only version, and trust the Holy Spirit to open the person's eyes to the truth of it all. What a moment that is. Here's what I told the Chinese doctor, something I learned many years ago through Child Evangelism Fellowship, (www.cefonline.com). There are five simple points, one for each finger:

> I have sinned (Rom. 3:23)
> God loves me (John 3:16; Gal. 2:20)

Christ died for me (1 Pet. 2:24; 1 Cor. 15:3)
I now receive Him personally (John 1:12; Rev. 3:20

I now have eternal life (John 3:16; Rom. 6:23)

Each of the five points has to be explained simply and clearly after reading aloud these verses. Through my translator, I went over this several times with the Chinese doctor. Having gone over the five points, ask the person to pray with you, to take the step of faith and trust Christ as personal Saviour and Lord. That may sound rather technical but remember, if I care I will communicate.

We are not here to argue with people. We can certainly dialogue with them and if there is genuine interest, talk over the real issues and in that process help them focus on Jesus, the Son of God, the only way to God (John 14:6; 1 Timothy 2:5-6).

Prayerfulness—This is all-important. One of the most amazing things I have discovered over the years is that God chooses to work through the prayers of His people. There is absolutely no substitute for the prayerful study of God's Word. Through this, the entire prayer life is set alight by the Holy Spirit; praying for people who need to know Jesus becomes so much more effective. Trust me, when you are prayerfully studying your Bible and, as a result, praying for people with a far greater passion, things change. You change. You will be filled with a far more genuine love and concern for those in your life. The Holy Spirit will open all kinds of opportunities for you to tell your story, for you to tell the people you are praying for them. The Holy Spirit will also prepare the people you are praying for to receive what you have to tell them. This is part of praying in the Spirit (Eph. 6:18).

Another exciting way of sharing with your world what God is doing in your life through your prayerful reading and study of His Word, is simply praying with people. You may be in conversation with someone who, for some reason unknown to them, begins to share a deep problem with you. This is to be expected when you have the glory of God upon your life. Many times I have seen all kinds of barriers broken down simply by gently offering to pray for and with that individual. I have done this in all kinds of situations. The response usually is one of amazement that anyone would care enough to pray with them. There is something so powerful about lifting up a situation to God. In doing this, you have made a friend and have opened a door to tell about God's love.

If you know someone who is in hospital, you don't have to be a full-time pastor to visit. Ask God to give you some scripture to share, maybe just a brief phrase. Leave it with them and pray with them briefly. The last thing you want to do is to embarrass a person in hospital. If the patient is not a Christian, you can simply leave that phrase from God's Word with them, assuring them you will pray for them. You may feel free to ask if they would like you to pray with them there. What you must not do is preach at them. It is an abuse of an opportunity to take advantage of someone who is weak. Never preach at someone in your prayer. When praying, you are talking to God on behalf of the patient, you are not talking to the patient on God's behalf.

Recently, I was doing this kind of visiting, not so much to hospitals but to people in their homes. I took my friend Bert and we discovered he had a real aptitude for this kind of ministry. He is continuing on his own. Bert loves Jesus and spends time daily in God's Word.

A Challenge

As you get into God's Word, are you willing to ask God to prepare you to be ready to pass what you are learning about Him to other people?

Something to Ponder

Who in your world ought you to be praying for with a willingness to tell them about Jesus as God gives you the opportunity?

THIRTEEN

The Bible and Preaching

I include this chapter because it is so important for the Jesus-follower to belong to a church where the Word of God is faithfully taught. If that is not happening in your present church you need to find another church. I spoke to someone the other day who had belonged to a church where, after talking about the events of Easter, the preacher told his people it was all a myth. That person did the right thing in finding a truly Bible believing church.

True biblical preaching has been known to empty churches because those in the pews did not want to hear the challenges from God's Word. This is the case where the professed Christianity is nothing more than religiosity. When God's ancient people, the Israelites, were in a situation of rebellion against God, they did everything they could to silence the true prophets. They only listened to those who told them what they wanted to hear. However, the opposite is more usual today — where the Word of God is preached with passion and a Holy Spirit anointing, the churches are full. Being popular has absolutely nothing to do with being a faithful preacher of God's Word. Having God's approval and being faithful to the text of Scripture is all-important. What matters is what people need, not what they want. In today's world, as much as at any other time in the history of the church, the people need to hear from God, not from men or women.

I once read that a preacher needs the head of a father, the

heart of a mother, and the hide of a rhinoceros.[18] Such a preacher will learn to be less concerned about what people think or say about him and more concerned to be obedient to the Holy Spirit in his preaching because he will have a heartfelt understanding and care for the people. He will be accountable to godly leaders who are over him in the Lord. Paul had exactly this attitude: *"we proved to be gentle among you, as a nursing mother tenderly cares for her own children."* Later he added, *"We were exhorting and encouraging and imploring each one of you as a father would his own children"* (1 Thess. 2:5, 11).

To Preach Is to Be Scriptural

Some today hold the view that preaching is outdated, a thing of the past. When one sees what happens when God's Word is preached with the anointing of the Holy Spirit, such thinking is obviously faulty. God owns such preaching and lives are changed; the hearers feel they have been fed in the deepest areas of their lives. That is because preaching is something God has ordained as the means of communicating His truth. Paul tells us, *"God was well pleased through the foolishness of the message preached to save those who believe"* (1 Cor. 1:21). Again he says, in his last letter, which gives the matter added urgency, *"I solemnly charge you in the presence of God and of Christ Jesus, who is to judge the living and the dead, and by His appearing and His kingdom: preach the word; be ready in season and out of season; reprove, rebuke, exhort, with great patience and instruction"* (2 Tim. 4:1-2). This conviction was so deep Paul was led to say, *"Woe is me if I do not preach the gospel"* (1 Cor. 9:16). Preaching the gospel means staying with the main theme of all of Scripture, Christ Himself. That is why Paul sums up his ministry by saying, *"We preach Christ crucified"* (1 Cor. 1:23). Oswald Chambers speaks to this so well when he says,

> "If we get away from brooding on the tragedy of God upon the cross in our preaching, it produces nothing. It does not convey the energy of

18 George Henderson, *Lectures to Young Preachers,* (B. McCall Barbour, Edinburgh)

God to man; it may be interesting but it has no power. But preach the cross and the energy of God is let loose."[19]

The preacher is not at liberty to preach opinions or to water down God's truth. His calling is to preach only the Word of God. Being true to the text of Scripture is his main concern, having applied the clear principles of hermeneutics (the interpretation of Scripture). It will then be applied to the people's lives out of the clear understanding of what it says and means. Having done his homework, the preacher will agonize in prayer over what the Holy Spirit has taught him in the Scripture, to be sure of what God's special word is for any given occasion. His main concern will be that he stands before the people with no selfish agendas, no unconfessed or unforgiven sin, being full of the Holy Spirit, and with the anointing of God upon what he is about to do. There is an important reason for this, as Paul makes so clear: *"My message and my preaching were not in persuasive words of wisdom, but in demonstration of the Spirit and of power, so that your faith would not rest on the wisdom of men but on the power of God"* (1 Cor. 2:4-5). Just because Christians may be having a good time in energetic worship is not necessarily an indication of God's power being among them. But when the preaching of God's Word is resulting in changed lives, and those lives become salt and light in their world the other six days of the week, making a difference for God's glory, the power of God is evident. When the preaching of God's Word is resulting in the people making themselves totally available to the Lord to go to wherever He wants to send them in the world carrying the gospel, then it is preaching with power. When a church has the vision to be a missionary-sending church and the leadership has the discernment to identify those God is calling to go, the preaching is with power. When people are coming to faith in Christ, obeying Him in baptism, and living transformed lives, and when this is happening on a regular basis, the power of God is evident. Think about it. What would you and your church be like if the Word of God were re-discovered and a new anointing

---

19   Oswald Chambers, *"My Utmost for His Highest"*—November 25th

came upon your life and on the preaching you hear regularly? Nothing is more important. Someone said many years ago, "If everyone in my church were just like me, what kind of place would my church be?"

Dr. Martin Lloyd-Jones, writing about the primacy of preaching, shows that,

> "The decadent periods and eras in the history of the church have always been those periods when preaching has declined. And, of course, when the Reformation and the Revival come, they have always led to great and notable periods of the greatest preaching that the church has ever known."[20]

Preachers Are Gifted by God

At the risk of sounding cliché, let me say preaching is not something a man just decides to do. Nor does he go to seminary to become a preacher. He goes because he already is one and his training is to help develop his God-given gift. No one should ever become a preacher because he can't get a job somewhere else or because he feels like a change of career. Being a preacher of God's Word should never be viewed as a job. It is a high and holy calling that ought never to be embarked upon apart from the overwhelming sense of having been called by God. Being called by God involves much more than just the person feeling the call. It involves other spiritually mature believers who know the would-be preacher well. How then is one to be sure of a call to preach God's Word? Some important guidelines:

A preacher is a disciple. It is evident from the preceding chapters that, if being a Christian means anything, it means coming into a master/disciple relationship with the Lord Jesus Christ. This means one's whole life is submitted to His authority. Growing in that relationship means coming to the place where

---

20 D. Martin Lloyd-Jones, "Preaching and Preachers" (Hodder & Stoughton) 24,25

the Master's will for the disciple becomes paramount. The disciple is totally available to his Master, recognizing he has no rights of his own. All of his life is submitted to the will of the Lord Jesus. There is simply no other way to bring glory to God. As Paul puts it, *"Do you not know that your body is a temple of the Holy Spirit who is in you, whom you have from God, and that you are not your own? For you have been bought with a price: therefore glorify God in your body"* (1 Cor. 6:19-20). Anything a Christian does in his or her own strength and not in the power of the Holy Spirit who lives inside his or her body, will never bring glory to the Lord. Jesus is the head of His body, the church, and Lord of the harvest. If I were to decide to become a preacher for any other reason than being clearly called by my Lord and Master, I am wasting His time, my time, and everyone else's time.

Every preacher goes through difficult times for various reasons but it needs to be said that it is very soon evident to anyone with spiritual discernment when a preacher is operating in his own strength and not in the power of the Holy Spirit. Only disciples are Spirit-filled because disciples are totally available to their Lord and Master.

A preacher is inwardly convinced of God's call. The personal and inward aspect of the preacher's call is the result of a growing and vital relationship with the Lord Jesus. The whole idea of becoming a preacher will begin in the preacher's heart. The Holy Spirit will begin something the real preacher will not be able to escape. The sense of being called begins in his heart and grows until he is compelled to do something about it. He may battle this growing conviction, putting up all kinds of reasons why he should not preach. If the call is real, he will be able to completely identify with Paul's words when he said, *"Woe is me if I do not preach the gospel"* (1 Cor. 9:16). He will feel he is totally unable to do anything else and be at peace. It came as a great shock to me as a young person struggling with the growing conviction of God's call to preach the gospel, when a senior and much-respected evangelist told me that if I could possibly avoid being a preacher, I ought to. I now know exactly what he was getting at and would not hesitate to say the same thing to any would-be preacher. Back then, however, it had the effect of driving me to my knees to continue wrestling out that matter in God's presence. A man truly called to preach will simply not be at peace doing anything else.

Other mature Christians will be involved in the call. We must never lose sight of why certain people are given, by God, as gifts to the church. In Ephesians 4:11-16, Paul teaches that those gifted people are there to help the rest of us be equipped for service. This is how Christ's body is built. Any of those five gifts (apostles, prophets, evangelists, pastors, teachers) who are only interested in building their own ministry or maintaining their position in ministry are failing miserably in what they are really called to do. Each ought to be on the lookout for others into whom they can pour themselves. They will discern where others are gifted and encourage the development of that gifting.

I am profoundly grateful to the late Alex Smith of Maddiston, Scotland, who saw some potential in me during my teenage years and provided me with opportunities to begin preaching. Such people will never know, this side of heaven, the value of that kind of encouragement. Rev. William Freel, B.D., PhD, came to preach in the church where I was a member, Olivet Evangelical Church in Falkirk, Scotland. He invited our young people to become involved with him in summer tent evangelism. I took up the invitation and the resulting experience led to the discovering and developing of the gift of God's grace to me to be a preacher of the gospel.

In Acts 13:1-4, there is the account of how mature and discerning leaders were involved in the call of Paul, or Saul as he was then, and Barnabas to be sent on the first great missionary journey. Those leaders came to recognize the hand of God on the lives of those two servants as they watched the work of the Holy Spirit in their lives. If the inward work of the Holy Spirit is truly happening in someone's life, it will be impossible to hide from spiritual leaders who are discerning and encouraging. It was the most encouraging thing in the process of my call when my church leadership, because they had nurtured what they felt to be a God-given gift, were willing to add their blessing and support.

A called preacher cares about people. The preacher is not preaching God's Word for the sake of it or because it is part of his job description. He realizes he is called to a high and holy calling; to prepare people for eternity and to nurture them *"so their faith would not rest on the wisdom of men but on the power of God"* (1 Cor. 2:5). He will see the people to whom he preaches God's Word as hungry for spiritual food, food that will cause them to grow. He will give the people life-changing nourishment. The fact that lost people are coming to life-changing faith in Christ and that Christians are obviously growing, can be a wonderful confirmation of the call to preach. Such a preacher will not be interested in performing well but in feeding the hungry sheep.

He will have a passion to preach. Nothing in his ministry will be more important than his preaching ministry. If God has called and gifted an individual to preach His Word, that individual is free to concentrate on that calling. It is a huge mistake for the preacher to allow himself to be sidetracked from his primary calling by other things or people. He will have a deep understanding of the fact that the only thing that feeds people spiritually is the Word of God. Consequently, the main area in managing his time will be the study of God's Word. The preacher will strive to make sure the important remains important and is never invaded by the urgent. Feel the passion in Paul's words to the younger man, Timothy:

> *"Until I come, give attention to the public reading of scripture, to exhortation and teaching. Do not neglect the spiritual gift within you, which was bestowed on you through prophetic utterance with the laying on of hands by the presbytery. Take pains with these things; be absorbed in them, so that your progress will be evident to all. Pay close attention to yourself and to your teaching; persevere in these things, for as you do this you will ensure salvation both for yourself and for those who hear you"* (1 Tim. 4:13-16).

He will preach with passion. It is difficult to understand how any preacher, truly called by God, reveling in the richness of God's Word, aware God has given him a message for the people, having agonized in prayer over the message and the people, can do anything other than preach with passion. People immediately recognize passionate preaching that feeds their souls and they will come back for more.

The preacher's spouse must be totally supportive. It is impossible to put into words how important this is. There are many unusual demands made on the preacher's time. He and his family live a goldfish bowl kind of existence. Such a life is impossible (this is no exaggeration) if the spouse is not supportive. This ought to be a priority for the younger preacher, aware of God's call and contemplating marriage. The right marriage partner for the preacher is a priceless blessing. It would be far better for him to be single than married to an unsupportive wife. His God-given partner will be his staunchest prayer partner, his greatest encourager, his most discerning critic.

FOURTEEN

Beyond the Sacred Page

Knowing that your life is making a difference in your world is what gives impetus to getting out of bed each morning. Every human being has to have purpose, otherwise life loses its meaning. Not to have a reason for being is the end. There are people who give up because of that. All of us have times in our lives and careers which are less than satisfying. Every job has its boring parts but that is vastly different from a situation where life has no meaning. It must be unbelievably difficult to be constantly not wanting to get out of bed because you simply don't want to be in the job you are in. There is another way to look at things. What a difference it makes to think from the point of view of God's purpose for you rather than from the point of view of your purpose for yourself. God's purpose is nothing short of making a masterpiece out of you. He wants to make you like His Son, Jesus. God will stop at nothing to make that happen. When a person is truly His child, God's promise is to make everything that happens in life work toward that great end. Take time to meditate on Romans 8:28-29. There is nothing that can happen to the true follower of Jesus that God cannot take and cause to work for good.

Sometimes we have the privilege of meeting people who have been called upon to go through horrendous experiences. As they look back, they often say they would not have missed the experience for anything. God has taken tragedy and caused it to work for good. Several times in the New Testament, Paul says he would rather glory in his weaknesses so that the power of Christ would operate in his life (see 2 Cor. 12:9). This is why it is so vitally important to understand that a person's true identity has nothing to do with their career, their family, their wealth, or anything else. The true identity of the individual is in their relationship with God in Christ. That is the reason for being alive, that is what elevates the most mundane parts of life to the level of sanctified Christ-like living. I will never forget sitting by the bed of a dear friend just days before she died. The glory of the Lord was upon her as she said, "You have to be where I am to know how real God can be." For Mavis, life still had purpose, even as she faced death. She had that living hope of the true Christian in her heart. Her main purpose in life was not her beautiful new home, nor her happy marriage, nor her possessions, but Christ Himself. This went on through death into the full enjoyment of life eternal in His presence.

If you were to read this book and, as a result, get into the reading and study of God's Word, but only as a chore, the whole exercise would be a failure. I can't emphasize enough that the object of the exercise is to discover Christ in Scripture, to meet Him there, to worship Him there, to draw close to Him there. Never forget, Christ and God's great plan of salvation for the world through Him is the central theme of Scripture. Everything in the Old Testament points to Christ, the gospels are the historical revelation of who He is, the book of Acts demonstrates the transition into the church age, the letters and the Revelation contain teaching as to how to move toward the second coming of Christ. It is Christ from beginning to end—to miss this is to miss everything. One reason the Holy Spirit lives inside the believer in Jesus is so He can reveal Christ to that individual through Scripture. As Jesus put it in John 16:14, speaking of the Holy Spirit, *"He will glorify Me, for He will take of Mine and will disclose it to you."* There is a wonderful old hymn by Mary Lathbury which sums up all this so well:

> Break Thou the bread of life,
>   Dear Lord to me,
> As Thou didst break the loaves
>   Beside the sea;

Beyond the sacred page
 I seek Thee Lord;
My spirit longs for Thee,
 Thou living Word.

The great apostle Paul, author of most of the New Testament letters, was passionate about this. He was trained in all the Old Testament law to the extent of being able to call himself a Pharisee. That meant he was more committed than any other group among his people, the Jews, to learning and practising God's law. The day he met the risen Jesus while on a journey to Damascus changed everything. He tells us in Philippians 3 that all his Jewish pedigree, his training, and his great learning, was rubbish compared to the surpassing value of knowing Christ Jesus his Lord. It takes a deep work of God's Holy Spirit to produce this kind of passion in the heart of a Christian. How I pray, even as I write, that God would so work in us all, as His people, to produce a passionate hunger to know Jesus through the God-breathed Scripture. Something of Paul's passion comes through in Philippians 3:10, *"That I may know Him and the power of His resurrection and the fellowship of His sufferings, being conformed to His death; in order that I may attain to the resurrection from the dead."* God's purpose for each Christian is to live in resurrection life. That is Christ's life, and it only happens as Christ lives His life in the Christian, and so through the Christian. This is why the Bible describes a true Christian as a new creature (2 Cor. 5:17).

It is a contradiction in terms for anyone to call themselves a Christian and still not be free from their past. Once a person has come in true repentance and faith to the cross where Jesus died, where He fully and finally dealt with all our sin and guilt, that person is totally free. It is now a question of realizing that the old self with all its sin, failure, guilt, and fear is dead, crucified with Christ (Gal. 2:20). It is now a question of believing God and not all the nagging hang-ups from the past. Whatever my family background, whatever others may have done to me, whatever attitudes I may have adopted as a result, in Christ I am now totally free. I have the choice of listening to the voice of God in His Word or the voice of my past with all its accusations that I'm a failure and not good enough or that I don't deserve to be free.

None of us deserve anything of what God wants us to enjoy in Christ. That is what the grace of God is all about. It's about us receiving what we do not deserve. It is time for all of us to stop making excuses for ourselves and our failures. It is time to stop blaming others and to stop hiding behind our past, finding a warped sense of security. Some of us do that because we realize that doing otherwise means admitting we are wrong and stepping out of what we have hung on to for so long. The devil has convinced some of us that if we did that, we might fall flat, that we could not handle the new person we would become. Worse, he has us asking ourselves, what if people who have become used to us the way we are do not like the new person we will become? It is not for nothing that the Bible describes the devil as the accuser of the brethren (Rev. 12:10). That verse makes clear the devil has been thrown down and that those who overcame him did so *"because of the blood of the Lamb and because of the word of their testimony."* They overcame because they stood firmly on what Jesus did for them at the cross. They saw His blood as their only plea before God because it and it alone dealt with all that sin means and all that sin has done. It's called being redeemed, set free, liberated in Christ forever. The word of testimony is telling the devil that all his accusations are groundless: "I am not the person I was, I am a new creation in Christ! I refuse to listen to your accusations. I choose to believe God and move forward in His power." Jesus said of the devil *"there is no truth in him"* (John 8:44) and that, *"Whenever the devil speaks a lie, he speaks from his own nature, for he is a liar and the father of lies."* Nothing the devil says is to be believed. Have you ever thought that listening to his lies and accusations is so wrong and grieving to the Holy Spirit?

It is a huge moment when we face our past and failures with total honesty, no longer making excuses. We then realize it was for all those failures and excuses that Jesus died and we come in brokenness and self-humbling to the cross and let it all go. We lay it down and totally relinquish it to Him. What a moment of release. A whole new future opens and what we imagined as the worst thing that could ever happen, having to truly face reality, becomes the greatest thing to ever happen. It becomes a moment for which we thank God from our hearts for the rest of our lives.

This is why meeting Jesus in the Word of God is all-important. If you are not meeting Him there, seeing His glory and growing in your relationship with Him, you will simply become more embroiled in religiosity. You will never get beyond the trappings of your faith, you will never be free to be the Christ-like person God wants you to be. Don't be like the man on the cruise ship who was found standing on deck eating crackers and cheese, because he failed to realize that having a ticket meant he could enjoy everything available on the cruise ship to the full.

In an earlier chapter, it was made clear what is involved in the study of any particular part of God's Word. All of it is vitally important, but there are dangers to avoid. It has been well said many times that becoming a committed Christian does not involve committing intellectual suicide. In all our study of God's Word, we must be diligent to be intellectually honest. All God's truth must reach the heart but always through the mind. The danger to avoid, however, is that of allowing the truth we are learning to stop at the brain and never reach the heart. Therefore, there is a time when the commentaries and other study books are laid aside and we get on our knees in God's presence and ask the Lord what He, not the scholars, wants to say to us. This is when we will experience having the Holy Spirit as our teacher. Our prayer life will take on a whole new meaning. We will find ourselves pouring out our hearts to God in worship, adoration, and prayer. This kind of private devotion and worship always leads to much more qualitative, corporate adoration and worship. People who meet God in His Word, Monday through Saturday, truly worship Him on Sunday. Their hearts are so full, they can't help but worship.

Never lose sight of the two main ingredients in meaningful study of God-breathed Scripture. They are:

Faith—trusting God and taking Him at His word.

Obedience—demonstrating trust by acting upon what is revealed by the Holy Spirit.

Something to Ponder

The Cross

C—cancels sin; Colossians 2:13-14

R—removes guilt; Hebrews 9:14

O—opens the way to God; Ephesians 2:12-18

S—separates from sin; Galatians 6:14

S—sets apart for God; Mark 8:34-38

One Final Challenge

The moments you spend each day in God's Word are the most important ones of your day. Having read this book, you are now faced with a choice to continue with mediocrity or to make Jesus Lord in your life and make time each day to meet Him in His Word. The results will be a transformed life, which means:

- Freedom from sin and the past
- A peace-filled mind and heart
- A more Christ-like lifestyle
- Greater freedom in telling other people about your Saviour
- A sense of purpose in life
- An assurance about your eternal home.

The choice is yours; the results, eternal.

End Notes

1. Derek Kidner, *Genesis—an Introduction and Commentary*, Tyndale, O.T. Commentaries, IVP.

2. F.F. Bruce, *The Epistle to the Hebrews*, New London Commentaries, Marshall, Morgan & Scott, p. 81,82.

3. J. I. Packer, *Fundamentalism and the Word of God*, (I.V.F), p. 77.

4. J. I. Packer, *Fundamentalism and the Word of God*, (I.V.F), p. 47.

5. Josh McDowell, *Evidence that Demands a verdict*, Campus Crusade for Christ.

6. William Lane Craig, *Reasonable Faith*, (Crossway Books)

7. J. I. Packer, *Fundamentalism and the Word of God"* (I.V.F), p. 66.

8. J. I. Packer, *Fundamentalism and the Word of God"* (I.V.F), p. 67.

9. Josh McDowell, *Evidence that Demands a Verdict*, Campus Crusade for Christ, p. 33.

10. John R.W. Stott, *God's New Society*, (I.V.P), p. 204.

11. John R.W. Stott, *God's New Society*, (I.V.P), p. 203.

12. Billy Graham, *Just As I Am*, Harper Collins, p. 137-140.

13. Keith Price, *Thirsting After God*, Christian Publications Inc.

14. Stephen Covey, *The Seven Habits of Highly Effective People*, Simon and Schuster.

15. Prof. James Denney, *The Death of Christ*, p. 84.

16. George Henderson, *Lectures to Young Preachers*, B. Mc-Call Barbour, Edinburgh.

17. Oswald Chambers, *My Utmost for His Highest*, November 25th.

18. D. Martin Lloyd-Jones, *Preaching and Preachers*, Hodder & Stoughton, p. 24, 25.

Enjoy Your Bible!
William MacDonald and Arthur Farstad
B-EYB

Studying God's Word should become a delight and a joy. This little volume is to help chart your own early excursions on the limitless seas of adventuring into the written Word of God.

To Order:
Toll Free: 1 800 952 2382

E-mail: orders@gospelfolio.com

Mail:
GOSPEL FOLIO PRESS
304 Killaly St. West,
Port Colborne ON L3K 6A6

Visit our Webstore where you can shop 24/7
www.gospelfolio.com

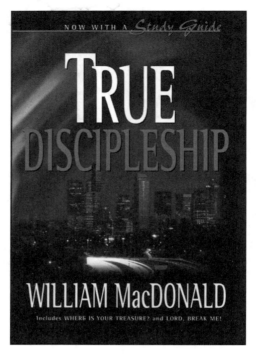

True Discipleship with Study Guide
William MacDonald
B-1917

This book clearly explains the principles of New Testament discipleship. The Saviour's terms of discipleship are not only highly practical but will reward in knowing the peace that passes understanding.

To Order:
Toll Free: 1 800 952 2382

E-mail: orders@gospelfolio.com

Mail:
GOSPEL FOLIO PRESS
304 Killaly St. West,
Port Colborne ON L3K 6A6

Visit our Webstore where you can shop 24/7
www.gospelfolio.com

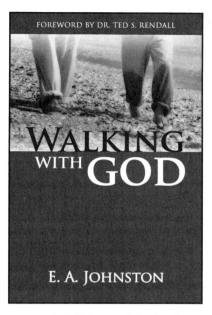

Walking with God
E. A. Johnston
B-7583

Is Walking With God Your Passion? As you read this book, be prepared to be counseled, corrected, convicted and challenged concerning your own walk with God. Learn some valuable lessons from Enoch. He was well pleasing to God, *"And Enoch walked with God"* (Gen. 5:24).

To Order:
Toll Free: 1 800 952 2382

E-mail: orders@gospelfolio.com

Mail:
GOSPEL FOLIO PRESS
304 Killaly St. West,
Port Colborne ON L3K 6A6

Visit our Webstore where you can shop 24/7

www.gospelfolio.com

Know the Book
Dr. E. A. Johnston
B-7337

A survey of each book of the Bible. At a glance the reader can grasp the central truths and content of each book. It is a helpful extra tool for Bible study or teaching.

To Order:
Toll Free: 1 800 952 2382

E-mail: orders@gospelfolio.com

Mail:
GOSPEL FOLIO PRESS
304 Killaly St. West,
Port Colborne ON L3K 6A6

Visit our Webstore where you can shop 24/7
www.gospelfolio.com